Laughing Matter II

Edited and Compiled

by

KAY BATCHELOR

and

KEITH MAYLIN

★ THE BOOK THEY'RE ALL TALKING ABOUT

IT PUT NEW HEART INTO ME — Christian Barnyard

HO HO HO — Father Christmas

A BIT OF A DRAG — Dinny LaRue

DIDN'T LIKE THE COLOURED CARTOONS — Enos Powell

MUCH BETTER THAN PEANUTS — Jim Carter

WOULD HAVE LIKED TO SEE MORE NUDES — Patsy Whitehouse

SOME VERY FUNNY TALES — Basil Brush

I LAUGHED TILL I BUST — Racquet Welsh

SOME OF THE JOKES WERE A BIT NEAR THE KNUCKLE — The Butchers Gazette

IT WAS NEWS TO ME — Angela Rippoff

IT WAS A KNOCK—OUT — Mohammit Dali

LIKED THE PICTURES BUT DIDN'T UNDERSTAND THE WORDS — A. Einstein

A LOAD OF OLD RUBBISH — GLC Dustman

THIS IS SOMETHING WE ALL NEED AND DON'T GET ENOUGH OF — Belinda Lovelace

NOT LEWD ENOUGH BY HALF — Lord Shortford

HAD ME ROLLING IN THE AISLES— Archbishop of Kanterbury

THE ONLY BOOK TO NOMINATED FOR
5 OSCARS, 3 CHARLIES, 2 JIMS and a GERTIE

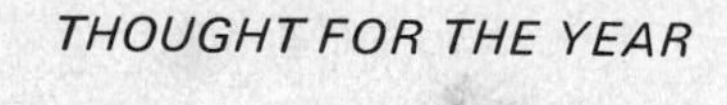

THOUGHT FOR THE YEAR

And lo, I heard a voice say unto me —
"Smile things could be worse."
So I smiled — and they got worse!

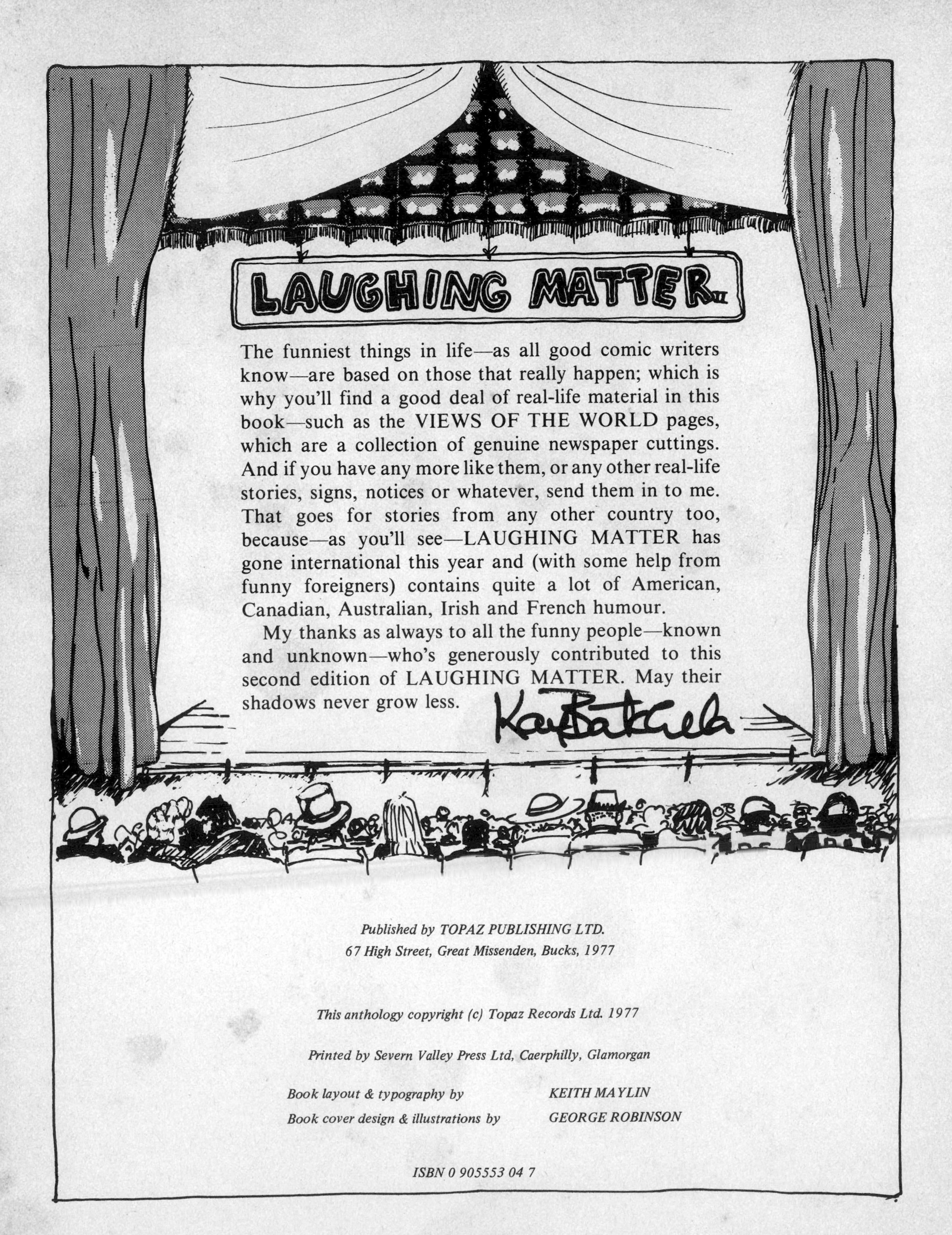

The funniest things in life—as all good comic writers know—are based on those that really happen; which is why you'll find a good deal of real-life material in this book—such as the VIEWS OF THE WORLD pages, which are a collection of genuine newspaper cuttings. And if you have any more like them, or any other real-life stories, signs, notices or whatever, send them in to me. That goes for stories from any other country too, because—as you'll see—LAUGHING MATTER has gone international this year and (with some help from funny foreigners) contains quite a lot of American, Canadian, Australian, Irish and French humour.

My thanks as always to all the funny people—known and unknown—who's generously contributed to this second edition of LAUGHING MATTER. May their shadows never grow less.

Published by TOPAZ PUBLISHING LTD.
67 High Street, Great Missenden, Bucks, 1977

Printed by Severn Valley Press Ltd, Caerphilly, Glamorgan

Book layout & typography by KEITH MAYLIN
Book cover design & illustrations by GEORGE ROBINSON

ISBN 0 905553 04 7

VIEWS OF THE WORLD

IN THE CHRISTMAS SPIRIT

Last Christmas Eve the Tuckers asked the Frys to supper. In the course of the evening Mr Fry gave Mrs Tucker an extravagant kiss under the mistletoe.

This upset Mr Tucker who ran out of the house and threw himself under a passing car.

Seeing his friend lying in the street Mr Fry took an overdose of sleeping pills while Mrs Fry called an ambulance.

When the ambulance arrived — with the police — Mrs Tucker was helping Mr Fry (who had collapsed in the hall) to take more sleeping pills, and Mrs Fry was calling a doctor.

Inspector Callicot tried to take the pills away from Mrs Tucker, who kicked him in the shins for his pains. As Sergeant Courtney Browne went to his Inspector's rescue, Mr Tucker — who had survived the car incident — punched him in the eye for assaulting his wife, while that lady removed her shoe and redoubled her attack on Inspector Callicot.

The ambulance men, excited by the melee, joined in but failed to stop Mrs Tucker driving the Inspector into the bathroom and pushing him into the bath which was filled with vodka.

Mrs Tucker, aged 18, was fined £80.

Underground Movement

An Australian lady driving her two young sons from Sydney to Melbourne found the road surface inferior. Thinking that she had taken a minor road she decided to push on and hope for the best. In any case it was pitch dark. She felt safer in the car.

A few minutes later the front of her car struck something like a tree.

Getting out to investigate she found she had driven half a mile into a coal mine. She and her sons emerged six hours later.

Passengers Request Stop

Complaints from passengers wishing to use the Bagnall to Greenfields bus service that "the drivers were speeding past queues of up to 30 people with a smile and a wave of the hand", have been met by a statement pointing out that "it is impossible for the drivers to keep their timetable if they have to stop for passengers".

Canine Capers

Shortly after they returned to Haslar Close, Mr and Mrs Laden of No. 12 became involved in an argument over the chances of a man overcoming a dog.

"We invited Harry Porter of No. 7 to have a nightcap," said Mr Laden. "Out of nowhere we began to argue about men beating dogs in a series of straight fights. Suddenly, Mr Porter leapt out of his chair and shouted, 'I'll prove it', as he jumped onto Bullseye, my wife's Irish terrier."

"Luckily for Porter," Mr Laden continued, "Bullseye was sound asleep."

Mr Porter, who appeared in court with a bandage around his head, said: "I never touched their part-terrier dog. I straddled him and gave a low growl. Then one of them hit me with a poker."

CURRY EATING SPECIALIST FINED FIVE POUNDS

A stranger in an Indian restaurant in Southend tried to demonstrate to Mr Arthur Flint how he should eat his curried chicken and rice, Mr Flint demonstrated his displeasure by pushing the curry in his face. In return, Mr Flint received a blow on the head with a chair.

At Southend court today the stranger, William Parkins, aged 28, a paint colour matcher, of Boston Avenue, Southend, pleaded guilty to assaulting Mr Flint and was fined £5 with £3 3s. costs. Mr R. A. Shorter, prosecuting, said Mr Flint and a friend had ordered a meal when Parkins, sitting at a nearby table, spoke to them. He sat down uninvited and advised Mr Flint to drink a glass of water before eating the curry. Then he said he would show him how to prepare the meal, picked up the rice and poured it on the curry, and mixed it together. Mr Flint sat watching and then asked: 'Have you finished?' Mr Parkins said he had, whereupon Mr Flint picked up the plate and pushed it into his face.

The curry and rice ran down Parkins's clothing and following an argument, he left. Later, as Mr Flint sat eating a replaced meal, he felt a severe blow on the head and shoulders and on grappling with his assailant, found he had caught hold of the curry-stained Parkins. Police were called and Parkins told them: 'I hit him with a chair. My pride couldn't take it. He pushed me too far.'

In a statement he explained that he was only showing Mr Flint how to prepare his meal and added: 'He picked up the plate and pushed the whole lot in my face. I was shocked beyond belief because he seemed so friendly.'

New Measures to Control Traffic

WHILE demonstrating Djakarta's new computer-controlled traffic regulation scheme, Mr Ali Sadkin, the city's governor, said that the electronic clerk had cost £2 million and that: "All the traffic policemen of Djakarta have been issued with stones which they have been ordered to throw at drivers ignoring the new rules."

LOVERS LEAP

Soon after the wedding of Mr Stanislaus Lembke to his bride Katharina had begun, the guests noticed that the groom looked miserable. When the priest came to that part of the service in which the couple are reminded of their future marital responsibilities, Stanislaus rushed out of the church and threw himself into the river Danube.

"I can't understand what came over him," said Katharina.

LITTLE ONES

BUT MUMMY I HAD TO, IT'S GOT RABIES!

The best thing about children — give or take a few features — is that they don't change. I mean, going back to school and watching the kids go in, aren't they the same lot you used to charge through the gates with? The clothes may vary (and how!), and the hairstyles (or lack of them), the slang, and the latest in everything, BUT the ghastly jokes are the same, the cloakroom graffitti unaltered, and the tribal secretive world just as warm and savage as it was when we were in it.

*Children are also MORE of everything than we are. Early on they're hair-raisingly honest (adults call this rudeness — especially if the little horror has just described someone as "really quite old", takes a hard look at you and adds "nearly as old as you I should think.") They're also unconsciously funny, like the little boy who wept to find he'd only got two testicles because he thought that meant he could only make two babies in his entire life. (***Batchelor's Belief No. 4b:** *no one starts being* **deliberately** *funny until they begin shaving or counting their spots). Above all, children are irreplaceable. That is a nice ambiguous statement which can either mean you don't know what you'd do without them, or — who needs 'em.*

K.B.

What Dr SPOCK didnt tell us

TARZAN'S GLUT

A dietary hallucination occurring when a baby is allowed to feed himself at too early an age. In this, the baby sees all this food as alive and believes that it must be killed before it can be devoured. Given a piece of cake, a nine-month-old baby, before putting it in his mouth, will either strangle it or beat it to death. Strangling is the more common of the two techniques and only when the cake is shooting out between his fingers does he consider it dead enough to eat.

To properly eat a piece of cake the baby should screw it into his mouth but invariably he will attempt to put it in sideways, resulting in an earful of crumbs and an iced nostril. The baby who prefers beating his food to death is generally considered the more savage and should never be left alone with kittens, puppies or fathers. This child's favourite food is a jam sandwich. Invariably he will place the sandwich upon the highchair tray and, in a flash, give it a murderous whack with the flat of his hand. As the jam quite often shoots some thirty feet, this child is popular only with ants, dogs and linoleum salesmen.

GLENN'S EXIT

A psychic phenomenon in which a small boy will be around the house for hours but, within ten seconds of being called for a meal or a job, will, for all practical purposes, disappear from the face of the earth. Occurs always in conjunction with *Laggard's Ear*. The boy, though normally possessed of a sense of hearing that enables him to detect the tinkle of an ice-cream vans bell five miles away, will, on this occasion, lose the use of both ears and, though no farther away than the next yard, will be unable to hear his own name called, no matter how many times or how eloquently his mother bellows it.

DURANTE'S FRENZY

A violent thrashing of a baby's arms, legs, head, feet, rib cage and buttocks, punctuated by shrieks from the baby and profane mutterings from attendant parents seeking to control the thrashing. Caused by belief among babies that the human nose is a fit depository for anything but nose drops. The average eighteen-month-old will, without a qualm, introduce into his nostrils peas, marbles, collar buttons, cigarette butts and carpet tacks, but when asked to submit the same organ to four drops of nasal balm, immediately fears for his life, evidently confusing the nosedropper with a suctional device for removing the brains.

Administering the nose drops against the child's wishes is the equivalent of force-feeding a python and, unless the mother outweighs the child by 10 stone or has recourse to a vice, strait jacket and leg irons, the assistance of the father will be required. The father should first gird himself with ear muffs, raincoat and fencers mask, because in the ensuing struggle there is always considerable doubt as to who will wind up with the drops and where. In administering suppositories the father should exercise even more care.

VISITOR'S TRANCE

A hypnotic state into which a child will fall upon occasions when his parents have visitors. Though the parents themselves may regard the visitors as the biggest bores in ten counties, the child seemingly regards them as circus performers in disguise, who at any moment will sprout funny hats and start squirting one another with soda syphons. Thus entranced, he will remain underfoot, staring and hanging on their every word, until such time as he is forcibly ejected from the room by whichever parent he has made the most nervous. Unfortunately, the ejection seldom takes place in time to prevent an attack of *Big Mouth's Hospitality,* in which the child, in a loud voice, asks if the visitors can't stay for dinner.

BUTT'S DISEASE

A malignant oiliness of the tongue in which an older child, accused of tormenting a brother or sister, will always start her defence with the words, "But all I did was . . ." These words, invariably uttered in profound amazement and innocence, are indicative of a brilliant but diabolical mind. The child has discovered how to cause a maximum of grief with a minimum of effort. Thus she will send a younger sister into a screaming tantrum and, upon the arrival of the mother on the scene, will pitifully protest, "But all I did was give her a little pat on the head!" She fails to add that she was fully aware of the fact that nothing irritates the victim as much as "a little pat on the head." As Paris, a pioneer in the field, remarked upon the occasion of Achilles' death: "But all I did was shoot him in the heel!"

HAMLET'S MANIA

A morbid fondness for death scenes; a temporary but violent hysteria in which an injured child, no matter how slight the injury, believes herself to be at the point of death and howls accordingly. These cries are accompanied by such elaborate dramatic effects that the father is immediately convinced that the child *is* at death's door and will race through the house, vaulting tables and crashing through unopened doors, going to her rescue.

A child falling down the front steps and slightly skinning a shin *could* hobble back into the house, but invariably she prefers *crawling* back, dragging her legs behind her. Her father, just as invariably, assumes that she has either been run over by a car or run down by a sex maniac. Just how quickly he can determine the true nature of the injury depends upon the child's capacity for the dramatic and fiendish. The child may want to milk the scene for all it's worth and for some minutes will refuse to divulge any of the details of the accident, parrying her father's queries by racing around the house and screeching. To reach a verdict in this case the father must either run her down or throw a tackle at her on her next swing through the living room.

Mothers, however, are very seldom victims of a child's dramatics, theorising that the louder a child hollers the less she is hurt. It is disgusting how often they are right.

EINSTEIN'S STUPIDITY

A form of mental seizure in which a child, eight years old or under, is rendered incapable of grasping even the most elementary aspects of time, speed, distance, etc. Upon leaving on a family holiday of 300 miles, the parent doing the driving will never get more than three miles beyond the city limits before the child is breathing down the back of his neck and asking, "How much farther?" No matter how simple an explanation is forthcoming, the question will continue to be asked on an average of once every ten miles throughout the trip, or until such time as the driver succumbs to apoplexy.

Dear God

WHY ISN'T MRS. GODS NAME IN THE BIBBLE ? WEREN'T YOU MARRIED TO HER WHEN YOU WROTE IT?

LARRY

I SORRY DID NOT WRITE BEFORE BUT I ONLY LEARNED HOW THIS WEEK

MARTHA

Dear God

We got a lot of religion in our house. So dont worry about us.

Teddy

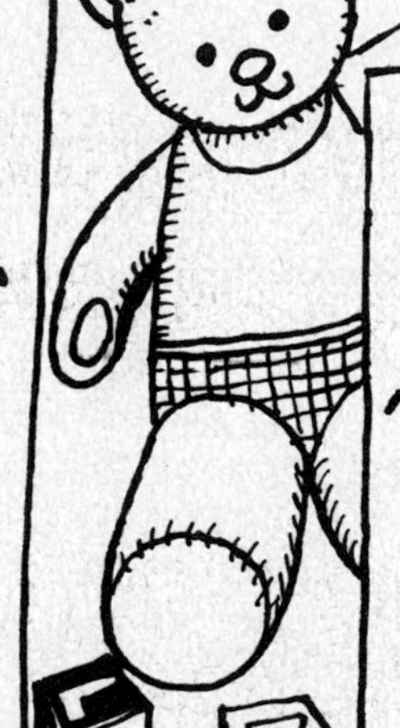

Dear God–

Please put another HOLiday between Christmas and EASTER. There is nothing good in there now.

Ginny

Dear God,

How come your never on T. V. ?

Kim

Dear God

When you make a miracel everybody says it is great, but I can't even play a trick without getting it.

allison

Reprinted by permission of A. D. Peters & Co. Ltd.

God help Us for We Knew the Worst Too Young

News that flying truancy squads have been set up by a number of police forces to catch absentee kids leads me to wonder where it will all go from there.

'PRISONER AT THE BAR, you are charged that on the afternoon of February 10, 1975, you did absent yourself without authority from Foskett Road Junior School, that when apprehended upon the premises of the Ram Gopal Fish and Takeaway Tandoori Parlour you told a whopping great fib, and that you were subsequently found to have in your possession a number of forged documents, to whit, a note ostensibly signed by your mother explaining that you were suffering from a bilious attack, a letter purporting to come from your doctor excusing you from school on the grounds that you had contracted bubonic plague from your cat, and a telegram signed by the Queen saying that it was a Muslim holiday. How do you plead?'

'Not guilty,' said a voice from a space between two policemen.

The judge leaned forward.

'Do you think,' he murmured, 'we could get him a box to stand on?'

A box having been brought, a small head appeared on the rim of the dock, and the counsel for the prosecution rose once more to his feet.

'Call Inspector Finch,' he said.

The court held its breath.

'I swear by Almighty God,' said the Inspector, 'that the evidence I shall . . .'

The judge leaned forward again.

'I think, perhaps,' he murmered, 'another box might be in order?'

After a minute or two, the Inspector's head emerged above the witness-box.

'. . . shall give shall be the truth, the whole truth, and nothing but the truth. Inspector Charles Finch, Truancy Squad, Q Division.'

The judge looked at him.

'I trust you will not take this as an intrusion, Inspector,' he said, 'but you appear to be considerably less than five feet tall.'

'Not considerably, m'lud,' said the Inspector. 'I would not say considerably. Marginally would be more the term I would select.'

The judge wrote something on his pad, carefully.

'If I might enlighten the court, my lord,' said the prosecuting counsel, 'there is no officer in the Truancy Squad above five feet in height. They are specially selected, my lord. Working as they do in plain clothes, under cover, as it were, mingling unnoticed with those base elements in our society which it is their duty to apprehend, it will readily be appreciated that the appropriate stature is of the utmost importance. A six-foot boy in a cap and short trousers might arouse suspicion, do you see?'

The judge nodded.

'He would dwarf his pencil-box,' he said. 'His, er, cover would be instantly, um, blown, I believe the word is, ha-ha-ha!'

'Ha-ha-ha!' shrieked the prosecuting counsel astutely. 'My lord tempers, as ever, wisdom and understanding with wonderful wit!'

'Toady!' cried the counsel for the defence, springing to his feet. 'Crawler! Judge's pet!'

'SILENCE!' roared the judge. He pushed his bifocals down his nose and stared at the defence counsel, most of whose head was enveloped in his wig, and whose gown covered his hands completely, and trailed on the floor. 'Am I to take it,' said the judge, 'that defence counsel in this case is also, begging the inspector's pardon, a midget?'

The prosecuting counsel cleared his throat.

'The prisoner, my lord,' he said, 'is represented by his friend Douglas. It is, as you I'm sure know, quite in order. *McKenzie's Friend,* my lord.'

'It is not in order for him to wear a wig,' replied the judge, 'if he is not a member of the Bar.'

'An attempt was made to remove the item from him, m'lud,' said the Clerk, 'but he bit us.'

'Serves you right!' shouted the defence counsel.

'Is counsel for the defence eating?' cried the judge.

'What if I am?'

'COME OUT HERE!' shouted the judge.

The counsel for the defence groped across the floor of the court, like a wounded bat, and put his boiled sweet on the edge of the judge's table. He paused on his returning shuffle, before the Clerk's bench.

'I want a receipt for that,' he said.

'May I continue, my lord?' said the prosecuting counsel. He turned to the tiny face of the Inspector. 'Do go on.'

The policeman flipped open his notebook.

'On the afternoon of February 10, 1975,' he said, 'I was on patrol, cruising along the pavement of Holloway Road, when I observed the prisoner through the window of the Ram Gopal Fish and Takeaway Tandoori Parlour. I parked my tricycle and approached. He was eating a piece of skate, and his side pocket contained what was clearly a folded school cap.'

'SNEAK!' cried the counsel for the defence.

'Approach the bench at once!' snapped the judge. He leaned forward, and smacked the defence counsel across the wig. 'One more interruption, and you will stay behind after court. Go on, Inspector.'

The Inspector cleared his throat behind a tiny, delicate hand.

'It was in the subsequent course of this conversation, that I was able to ascertain that the prisoner should at that moment have been doing tens and units with Miss Perrins at Foskett Road Junior School. I produced my warrant card and advised him of his rights.'

'What did the prisoner say?' asked the prosecuting counsel.

'He said I,' the Inspector held his book to the light and squinted at it, '. . . said I had a face like a dog's bum and he would get his gang on me and bash me up.'

The court gasped! A Chief Superintendent went pale! A jurywoman reached for the rail, and held on bravely!

'This gang,' muttered the judge, 'you know of them?'

'Oh, yes, my lord,' said the Inspector. 'They are known as the Black Daleks. They meet in a shed and have a special handshake and wear their caps backwards. It is rumoured that they bake their conkers, among other things, also put newts in girls' knickers, not to mention . . .'

'OBJECTION!' cried the counsel for the defence.

'No we never,' said the counsel for the defence. 'He is thinking of worms.'

'Overruled,' said the judge.

The prosecuting counsel rose.

'That is the case for the prosecution, my lord,' he said.

'I call the prisoner,' said the defence counsel.

The prisoner crossed to the witness box, and took the oath.

'Would you tell the court, in your own words,' said his counsel, 'exactly what your secret mission is?'

'Yes,' said the prisoner, 'provided they keep shut up about it. I think they ought to know I can kill people with a single Look.'

The judge took off his spectacles.

'What kind of look?' he said.

'I am not at liberty to divulge that, m'lud,' said the prisoner. 'But if you got it, you'd know.' He glanced about him, darkly. 'On the day in question, I was on a secret mission to stop the earth getting invaded by beings from outer space. There is a lot of this about, as everybody knows. I was sitting in the window of the fish shop disguised as an ordinary person eating skate, but really I was keeping watch for anything with nine legs, or green, or blatting anyone with their gamma guns, that sort of thing. It was while I was doing this that a midget came up to me, disguised as a boy, and began talking about Biffo the Bear.'

'How did you know,' asked the defence counsel, 'that he was a midget?'

'He had hair in his nostrils, and when you looked close you could see he had little tiny whiskers all over his face. We are trained,' and here the prisoner turned to the rapt jury, 'to notice these things. Also, any fool knows that Biffo the Bear has not been in the *Beano* for some years. It was just like when they drop Russian agents in places and the Russian agents go *What-ho, top-hole, jolly good, by Jove* and all that stuff, and you know they are really people called Ivan who've been mugging up Billy Bunter or somebody.

'You may step down,' said his counsel.

'No questions,' said the prosecution, wearily.

Whereupon, the summings-up having been eschewed, the jury filed out, filed back a minute or two later, and without a second's pause declared the prisoner Not Guilty.

Which, in view of the fact that they were twelve honest, stout, upstanding British citizens who had all previously written notes explaining that they would be unable to do jury service because of bilious attacks, nosebleeds, dying relatives, flat feet, indispensability at work, snow on the points, old war wounds and religious holidays, all of which had been refused point blank by the Sheriff, was hardly surprising.

This excerpt from 'Golfing For Cats' by Alan Coren (Robson Books Ltd.) was first published in Punch magazine.

The GENERATION GAP

"... and how's old Brucey then?"

"Strawberries! ... Millions of 'em!"

"Every time we come it's apple tart!"

"Mickey Thomson's Grandad's got a proper swimming pool, hasn't he?"

"... and this is your mummy on her pony—Binky its name was—when she was just your age."

"You know something, Grandpa ... Daddy says you're loaded."

Excerpts from 'All Other Men Have Mellowed' by Graham Published by Garnstone Press Ltd.

FAIRWAY TALE

by MICHAEL GREEN

Askew's seven-year-old daughter was recently asked to write an essay in school on the subject of sport. This was the result.

I am going to write about golf. My Daddy plays golf with Uncle Mike. Uncle Mike is very old, as old as Daddy. Uncle Mike has to play golf with my Daddy because he has no children of his own to keep him amused. I do not like Uncle Mike.

. . . One day Daddy took me to watch him play golf with Uncle Mike. Mummy made him do it as she had to have her hair done. Uncle Mike was not pleased and asked Daddy why he couldn't have left the brat at home, preferably in the kitchen with all the gas taps turned on.

When they got to the golf course they went into a little room in a big house and changed their clothes and then they came out and waited with a lot of other men while some others hit the ball. They were all old men too.

When a man hit a ball he said 'Shave off' and ran to one side to watch it hit the trees and all the others said, 'Ardluck, Charlie', but secretly I think they were pleased.

When Uncle Mike came to hit the ball he spent a long time waving his big club, and then he lifted it ever so high in the air and dug up a piece of earth with it and he was not pleased because he had been naughty and all the men looked at each other and said, 'Oh dear, what a naughty man.'

And I said, 'Are you digging for worms, Uncle Mike?' and they all laughed and one of them patted my head and said I was a clever girl, but I do not think Uncle Mike was pleased.

After Daddy had had his go he went into a little wood and Uncle Mike went into another little wood to look for their balls. Daddy found his ball under a bush. I got it out for him and he built a little mound of earth and put it on it and then he hit it out of the wood and went to help Uncle Mike who was looking into a drain.

I said to Uncle Mike, 'Daddy just found his ball under a bush and I got it out for him', and Daddy tried to put his hand over my mouth but Uncle Mike said I was a good girl and gave me a sweetie.

Then Uncle Mike found his ball and he hit it into the drain again and we had to wait while a lot of other men had their go.

Daddy did not go into the wood again but he took ever such a little club and he went to play in a sandpit like we have in the school playground only much bigger. Daddy played a lovely game throwing sand all over everywhere so I went into another sandpit next door and built a beautiful sand castle with a real moat.

When I showed it to Daddy he went very red and said, 'Good God, look what the child's done', and he and Uncle Mike went down on their hands and knees and flattened out my castle. While they were doing it a man came along on a sort of mowing machine and he said they ought to be ashamed of themselves and he would report them to the secretary, and Uncle Mike said that word again.

After that Daddy and Uncle Mike went to play on a little piece of flat ground with a lot of sandpits round it and a big stick in the middle and Daddy let me hold the stick. It was in a nasty little hole full of water. So when Uncle Mike hit his ball I stopped it from rolling into the nasty hole and Uncle Mike threw his club at Daddy and it hit him on the knee. Daddy said, 'You can't blame me for what the child does', and Uncle Mike said the only consolation was that I was as happy as if I was in my right senses.

Then we saw two lady golfers, and they were very old, as old as Mummy, and Uncle Mike said something to Daddy and they went away and whispered and came back laughing.

Then we came to a huge river and Daddy and Uncle Mike tried to see who could get most balls into it and my Daddy won because he hit the river more times, but he did not look pleased. Uncle

Mike said would I like to go and look in the river for the balls, preferably in the deepest part, but I did not go.

Then they went to play on a bit with a stick in the middle again. Daddy took out his teeny-weeny club, the one he uses to practice with in the living-room. He stood on the grass near the long stick, and he looked hard at the ball and hard at the long stick and then stood on one leg and then he started to breathe very heavily and then he asked Uncle Mike to stop blinking as the noise of his eyelids upset him.

Well, while Daddy was standing still and breathing hard I saw a squirrel and I whispered it to Uncle Mike, and he said, 'Go and tell Daddy now.' As Daddy was swinging his teeny-weeny club I ran up and I shouted, 'Daddy, Daddy, Daddy, I've just seen a squirrel', and he jumped and he hit the ball ever so hard, much harder than he hits it even with that big club with the lump on the end, and the ball went away into a sandpit.

Then Daddy went all sort of pale and trembly, like Diana Bradshaw when she was sick in the playground, and he kept twitching and muttering, and then he said, 'May God forgive me, but I want to kill my own daughter.'

Uncle Mike said would I pull his little truck for him as that might keep me quiet, and he let me pull the truck and I found it ever so easy and I ran round and round and round one of the long sticks just like a racetrack. But two nasty men came along and shouted at me and Uncle Mike took his little truck away from me and said if I had any more brains I would be half-witted.

Then we got back to where they started and we went into the big house and Daddy gave me a lemonade and Uncle Mike gave me sixpence and I put it into a big machine with coloured lights all over it, and I pressed a handle and a lot of sixpences came out of the bottom. Uncle Mike made a noise as if he was going to be ill and said it was the irony of life and now he had tasted the very dregs.

I shall not play golf when I grow up as it is a stupid, silly game. I told Mummy so when she was bathing me and she said I was quite right but men played it because they were silly, stupid people and Uncle Mike was the silliest and stupidest of them all.

Angela Askew (Form IV)

Excerpt from 'The Art of Coarse Golf'
Published by Curtis-Brown Ltd.

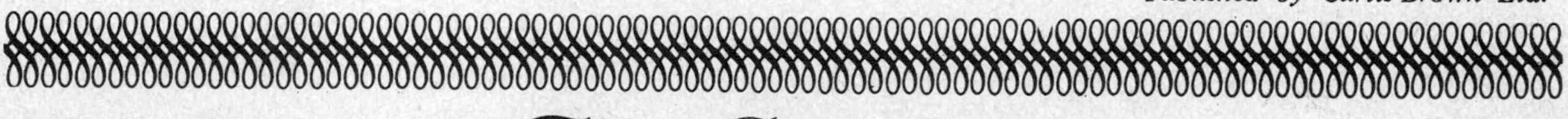

Written by Morris Dodd **The Perishers** *Drawn by Dennis Collins*

First Published by the Daily Mirror Newspapers Ltd

OUT OF THE MOUTHS OF . . .

Simon was making hard work eating some meat at his friend's house. The friend's Mother offered to help but he smiled sweetly and said, "It's OK— we often have meat as tough as this at home."

•

"Roger hit me" Simon wailed to his Daddy. "Why didn't you hit him back?" Daddy asked. "But I did," he cried "I hit him back first."

•

Simon was bursting to tell his mother about his first day at school. "I could answer every question" he beamed, "Good", said his mother, "and what did the teacher say?"
"Wrong" said Simon.

•

Sue unfortunately missed the special sex education at school but her friend was able to explain it to her "It's simple really, you just mix an egg with a bit of Spam."

•

Mummy was explaining her expanding middle to her daughter. The light began to dawn — "So that's where you keep the baby" said Sue "Is the pram in there too?"

•

When the baby was finally born the Vicar at the christening was teasing Sue, "Can I take your new baby brother with me", he asked. "Oh, no" she said sternly, "We brought him, you only wash him.

•

On the way home Sue studied her new baby brother and after some considerable time said to her mother, "He's not really very pretty is he? No wonder you hid him under your skirt all that time."

•

The children were having their tea when their mother heard a dreadful crash. "Have you broken that cup?" she shouted. "Well . . . only just a little bit of it." Simon answered hesitantly.

•

Sue was watching her mother applying her foundation cream. "Is that what you use to hide the cracks?" she asked.

•

Simon listened to the argument between his parents. When his Daddy had left the room he turned to his mother and wisely said, "Never mind, if we get a new one we'll get one that doesn't shout."

LESLIE (Virgin Soldiers) THOMAS

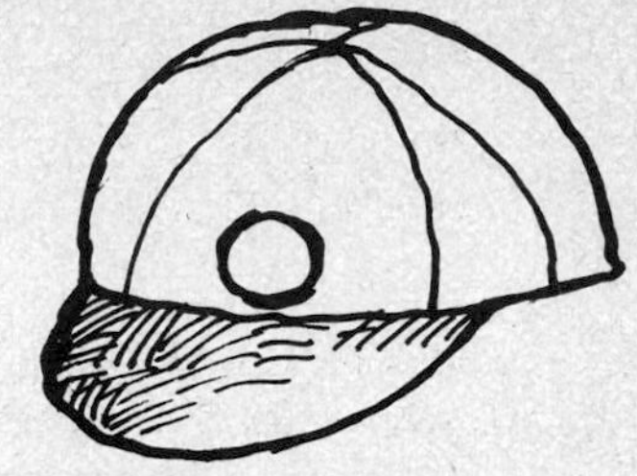

tells a hilarious story out of his less than hilarious childhood as a Dr. Barnardo's boy—

The Gaffer *("father" of Dickies the Home Leslie lived in)* was reading his paper when something drew him suddenly and he pounced at it like a bird spotting a morsel . . . and said "Thirty bob each. That's not bad is it?"

There was a mumble of agreement that whatever they were, at thirty bob each they weren't bad.

It turned out that the bargain he had perceived was a pair of goats. It was the first act in the introduction to Dickies of the nastiest, most conniving, vicious, stealthy, sly, sinful, and stinking inmates it had ever known.

Three of us he sent to collect his goats. I've never worked it out yet why he wanted the wretches. Probably because he was intensely patriotic, he imagined that if they had kids (as if he didn't have enough) he would be able to raise a goat herd and thus help the national war effort.

There was Grandpa, a melancholy youth with spinneys of hair cropping his face, and Frank Knights and myself.

We claimed the goats from a piggery somewhere beyond the river and Kingston Bridge. The three of us saw the animals for the first time and knew we were buying trouble. One was fawn and white and the other white. Both had pink, sleazy eyes and sniggering expressions. I have never looked upon two more debauched creatures. Unfortunately for the Gaffer's ambitions they never got around to having kids. They were both billies.

'We oughta brought the cart,' said Grandpa, dolefully regarding the animals. 'We'll never get 'em back.'

The cart referred to was a sturdy hand-barrow which nominally belonged to the Kingston cleansing department and was supposed to be used by road-sweepers. The Gaffer had borrowed it years before and had never got around to giving it back.

'We'll walk 'em—like dogs,' said Frank, who was one of the brainy kids in the home. 'Let's get some string.'

The crook who sold us the goats gave us the string and looked as though he was tempted to charge us for it. We tied it around the stiff hair of their necks and set off on the return journey.

At first it seemed that it was going to be smelly but non-violent. The putrid pair trotted along willingly.

'It's going to be simple as anything,' I said.

'Yerse,' muttered Grandpa. 'They're too shagged out to cause any bovver. Look at 'em.'

The bother came immediately they saw a trolleybus. It was going at a spanking pace and the white goat tried to get underneath it. It pulled Frank with a swift and decisive tug. He gallantly held the string, but the goat was going to do battle with the low snout of the trolley, and nothing was going to stop him.

Fortunately the bus driver had good reflexes. He hit his brakes ferociously; the ungainly vehicle skidded and stopped. When it stopped the goat, horns down, vile glint in the eye, was three inches from death. Frank was only a fraction further away. The conductor of the bus had fallen from the platform on to the road.

There was huge confusion. Traffic squealing, bus driver in a near faint, conductor rubbing his backside, passers-by giving advice and trying to tug the goat away from the trolleybus. In the middle of it all the goat I was holding, and which had remained placid, had a hearty pee all over my boots. So interested was I in the animated scene that my first awareness of this disgusting act was when the warm water trickled through the lace-holes and soaked my socks.

I cried out in horror and Grandpa, who was tugging the string of the other goat with Frank, turned and shouted: 'Wot you standing there for? Come and 'elp us.'

'I can't,' I bellowed. 'The thing's just pissed all over my boots.'

A man who had been laughing on the pavement sat down on the kerb and began to howl into his crossed arms. Everybody started laughing and Frank's goat, with two little jerky frisks, escaped and galloped away in the direction of Kingston Bridge. A whooping posse followed it, with the elongated Frank galloping bonily in the lead. At the bridge the goat stopped and looked around mildly as if wondering who was causing all the confusion. Frank regained the string, Grandpa held it with him, and I splashed up with my goat which until that time had been more insanitary than violent.

But there was time. At the centre of the bridge my goat tried to jump the parapet. There was a small stack of concrete tank traps, the sort that were hurriedly moulded everywhere during the invasion threat. They were piled like steps on the pavement offering an ideal scamper for this goat who must have had mountain ancestors. The creature ended up straddling the stone coping, forelegs over the river, hind legs over the pavement. In a red panic I released the string and grabbed two handfuls of the scrubby, stiff hairs on its back.

Frank and Grandpa, who were a few paces ahead, turned. 'It's trying to get into the river!' I cried.

'Let it,' said Grandpa stonily. 'Best place for the soddin' thing.'

Frank left Grandpa with the first goat and came to my aid. So did half a dozen passers by, several of whom had followed us from the last performance. A soldier got hold of the goat's tail and the animal began to bleat horribly. A gnome-like lady put down her shopping basket and began tweeting human instructions, an action which she later regretted since immediately we got the goat down it put one of its back legs into her basket.

People on the river and along the bank below, accustomed to seeing human heads peeping over, did a double-take when they observed this one.

Eventually we got it back and having had its moment of glory it seemed satiated and content to be led along. So did the other goat, apart from an abrupt and momentarily terrifying charge at a nun, and we triumphantly led them into Dickies.

The advent of this pair began a reign of terror. The Gaffer had them set free at first in the fenced-off, grassy area beyond the mud patch. But he knew more about boys than goats. The following day one was discovered truculently challenging the traffic in the middle of Kingston Hill and was returned by a policeman who said it could have caused a messy accident and should be tethered.

So the Gaffer had the goats tethered. They apparently liked their tethers because they ate them to the last strand and were next found pottering around the grounds of Kingston Hospital.

Chains were the next deterrent and they were more successful. But by industrious and secret tugging both animals were able to remove the stakes from the ground. Then they would break through, or go around, the fence and fly in fury across the mudpatch, over the playground, through the rooms and corridors scattering boys and staff.

'The goats are out!' the cry would ring. The Bulls of Pamplona caused no more scattering than this. Shrieks and shouts and tumblings. Down the Death Row passage they plunged once, with half a dozen boys just in front of their seeking horns and a hundred more shouting encouragement from behind. The pursued boys fled through the kitchen and gallant Mrs Mac tried to defend her territory with her ladle. But her bravery was brushed aside by the twin terrors who charged around and around the big table like tribal devils.

One of them—the white one—found a cloth in which some Dickies pudding had been steamed. It gobbled up the cloth and within the hour it was dead.

Boz, who had been on kitchen duties and had witnessed the entire drama, related it in the dormitory that night.

'After it 'et the puddin' cloth,' he said with relish, 'it laid down and sort of swelled up. We thought it was going to go off bang. Then it just conked out.'

'Fancy being killed by a Dickies' pudding cloth,' I remarked.

'It weren't the cloth,' said Boz scornfully. 'It was the bits of pudding that was sticking on it.'

The other goat lived for years. Its escapades continued after its partner's going, although it steered clear of the kitchen. In later years it became an embarrassment to a neighbour who would telephone and say: 'Your ruddy goat is in my outside lavatory again.' The goat one afternoon conscientiously trampled through every precious pane of his cucumber frame. He called and said something would have to be done. Mr. Vernon Paul, who had by this time become superintendent, with a stroke of native genius offered to give the goat to the neighbour as a present. The offer was promptly accepted.

It was, of course, more a case of giving the neighbour to the goat. The animal continued and insisted on spending most of his time in Dickies grounds, with occasional forays into the neighbour's garden, who was powerless to do anything since it was his goat. Soon he moved house and left the goat.

The animal grazed and grunted at Dickies for all of fifteen years. It was a dun-coloured patch on the landscape of the home familiar to generations of boys. When it died, it had a good and peaceful passing.

Excerpt from This Time Next Week Published by Constable & Co. Ltd.

LAW 'N ORDER

The law may be an ass (stand up the novelist who said that) but it takes a lot of laughing at sometimes — particularly when you're caught up in it yourself. It's hard enough not to be over-impressed just being on jury duty in a county court — where one of my fellow jurors was a pig-farmer absolutely frantic to return verdicts in one minute flat, because one of his sows was farrowing. And it wasn't easy to be quick, either, as most of our cases involved what the law salaciously calls "having carnal knowledge under the age of . . .", causing a lot of legal tee-hee about the girl in question looking "mature beyond her years, m'lud" and winning the tiniest tremor of a smile from the judge — who was definitely mature beyond **his** *years. Yellow with age, he was. And those wigs! Close to they looked like very old string that'd been yellowing on the garden shelf for years among the dried up beans and spiders' webs.*

In fact, the law is definitely yellow — skins, teeth, papers, double no parking lines, whites of prisoners' eyes (especially the drunk drivers). Even the lies aren't white in court.

K.B.

"Morning Judge. You know that advice you gave parents about if your boy abuses you hit him back......."

London Express Service

A man charged with stealing cars was told by the magistrate that he could be tried by his peers or be dealt with by him sitting alone: "What do you mean by peers?" asked the man and was told: "Peers are your equals, men of your own class and own kind". "You try the case on your own", promptly replied the accused, "I don't want to be tried by a bunch of car thieves".

At the Old Bailey an Irish labourer was being cross-examined at great length. Finally the judge asked his counsel: "Has your client never heard of the well-established doctrine 'Quamdiu se bene gesserit'?" Counsel replied: "With great respect, my Lord, when the boys gather on a Saturday night on the bogs of Ireland they talk of nothing else".

A policeman, on night duty, saw a stationary car outside a factory and being suspicious, waited beside it. A man came out shortly afterwards from the main gates and hurried into the car. The officer questioned him and asked him his name and address. The man gave his name as Mr. Cuddlebrake. The officer, not satisfied, decided to check the man's identity. He went to the gatekeeper and asked: "Have you got a Cuddlebrake here?" The gateman replied: "I don't know about that. It has taken us ten years to get a tea break".

A judge was asked what was the maximum penalty for bigamy and replied, "Two mothers-in-law".

The secretary of a wealthy American corporation consulted an eminent lawyer on a complicated trade question. The lawyer gave his answer with the single word "Yes". Shortly afterwards walking down 5th Avenue the secretary saw the lawyer, to whom he had just paid a very large consultation fee and said "Nice day". Before the lawyer had a chance to reply, the secretary added: "That's a statement, not a question".

A prisoner was acquitted and asked for costs. He said he knew he was innocent because he was in prison at the time. Asked why he did not say this during his trial, the man replied: "I thought it might prejudice my case".

A Maori engaged in a legal case was told by his lawyer that it was a case of his word against the other man's and the result would depend on which side the magistrate believed. The lawyer said: "If he believes your story, you win, but if he believes the other man's, he wins. It will depend upon your demeanour in the witness box". The Maori asked: "Will it help if I send the old beak along a brace of pheasants?" The lawyer answered: "If you do that it will be the end of your case". The Maori won his case and afterwards told the lawyer: "The brace of pheasants did the trick." The horrified lawyer cried: "Don't tell me you sent him a brace of pheasants?" And the Maori answered: "Yes, I sent them in the other man's name".

A doctor, a lawyer and a parson were shipwrecked on a desert island and the only chance of survival was for one of them to swim for help through a shark-infested sea. They drew lots and the lawyer lost. He set out with the other two watching him. Hundreds of sharks appeared but instead of attacking him they lined up on either side of him as an escort. The parson said it was a miracle and an answer to his prayers. The doctor observed: "It is merely an example of professional courtesy".

During a County Court hearing, the defendant cried out: "As God is my judge I do not owe the money". The Judge retorted: "He isn't. I am. You do. Pay up."

A client received his account and thinking it was heavy asked for an itemised break-down. The solicitor's itemised account included: "To recognising you in the street and crossing the busy road to talk to you to discuss your affairs and recrossing the road after discovering it was not you".

Gunfight at the OK Grill-Room

'High meat prices have made rustling highly lucrative, and it is increasing, says the National Farmers' Union. Livestock worth £30,000 was stolen last year. The NFU said another worrying development was that groups of townsmen were going out with .22 rifles to "kill themselves a sheep".'—Guardian

HE CAME OVER the ridge at sun-up, riding hard. He was tall in the saddle, and lean, and he was the law. He was grey with dust, and the grey was streaked with sweat, like a dry gulch veined briefly with morning dew before it burns off, cracking the parched soil again. It was a long ride out from town. At the top of the ridge, he dismounted, and took off his cycle-clips.

" 'Allo," he said, ' 'allo, 'allo.'

He was a man of few words. But he moved quicky, for a big man.

'Woss,' he said, 'all this, then?'

The two men crouching over the terrible remains looked up. He knew them. They farmed the area. They didn't say anything. They didn't need to. Not with what one of them was holding in his hands.

'That's a sheep's head,' said the lawman.

'That's right,' said the elder farmer.

'Very nice, boiled,' said the lawman. 'With a drop of vinegar.'

'It's the rest of the sheep we're worried about,' said the farmer's son.

'I'd roast that, personally,' said the lawman. 'Saddle, neck, best end, scrag—'

'It's gone,' said the farmer. 'Nothing left but the feet.'

'Ah,' said the lawman. His grey eyes narrowed to slits, and he stared at the bright horizon, thinking hard. 'Soup,' he said, at last.

'What?'

'From the feet. 'Course, you'll have to watch for ticks. Mind you, they tend to float out when it boils.'

The farmer stood up. His jaw was set.

'We want the man,' he said, 'who stole the carcase.'

The lawman took off his helmet, and squinted at the sun, and wiped the sweat from his forehead.

'I understand,' he said. 'There must have been a good forty dinners there.'

And, leaving them to ponder upon these telling words, the tall man threw a long leg over his saddle and rode back towards town.

The saloon fell quiet as his shadow slipped across the floor. Only the consumptive coughing of the hawkfaced doctor slumped at the cribbage-board punctuated the silence, as the sheepmen watched the man in blue walk to the bar, slow and easy.

'Stone's Ginger Wine,' he said.

The blonde barmaid piled her ravishing bust loosely upon the bar, and the thump of her golden heart rattled the glasses on the shelf behind her.

'That's five sheep gone this week, then,' she said.

'In a manner,' said the lawman, 'of speaking.'

'Why is it always bleeding sheep?' cried an embittered old solicitor from a far corner of the room, who had watched rustlers make nonsense of his subsidy from his far Holborn chambers, and had taken the unprecedented step of visiting his property, only to find his flock was a bucket of tails and an old ewe with croup.

'He's right!' exclaimed a young don, whose face was known to millions of TV fans and whose weekend cottage was now a mockery following the theft of the photogenic little lamb that had stood outside it in countless colour supplements. 'Why do they never steal cattle?'

The lawman turned, real slow, and fixed them all with his steely eye.

'What do you think, Doctor?' he said.

The hawkfaced man beat his heaving chest.

Ash fell from his cigarette. Liquor spilled from his glass. Cards flew from his sleeves.

'There's a lot of it about,' he wheezed at last. 'Take two—wurrgh!—take two aspirins and go to—aaaargh!—bed, and if it's no better, give me a—arf! arf!—ring in the morning.'

They all nodded. It was a small community. They owed him a lot.

'Never steal beef, do they?' said an ex-shepherd, forced now to open a discotheque. 'What kind of rustlers steals only sheep?'

They were still deliberating upon this, when the bar-doors flew suddenly open, and a distraught and trail-stained farm-worker hurled himself among them. His eyes were wild, and his trembling finger jabbed behind him.

'Come quick!' he croaked, and ran out again.

The lawman rushed after him, pausing only to fix his clips, sharpen his pencil, adjust his chinstrap, tune his whistle, and telephone the greengrocer. Within minutes, he was riding after the vanishing dot.

He caught him on the outskirts of town. The man was hiding behind a tree and pointing across open country to a cloud of moving dust.

'Rustlers!' he cried, as the lawman dismounted and began oiling his chain. He put his ear to the ground.

'Not making much noise,' said the lawman. 'You'd expect the thunder of hooves.'

'Not with chickens,' said the farm-worker.

The lawman looked again, It was true. A vast herd of Leghorns was galloping into the distance. Dimly, through the rising dust, they could make out the figure of a man on a moped, waving an umbrella to urge them on.

'Come on!' cried the farmworker.

The lawman sucked his lip, thumb in his belt, eye on the sun. He put up a wet finger, testing the wind.

'We'd best be off home, now,' he said. 'You can't never tell with chickens. Get in among that lot, you'd be pecked to ribbons before you knew it. It'll all be in my report, after my elevenses.'

'Chickens now,' said his wife. 'First sheep, now chickens. No beef.' She wrung out the tea-bag and put it back in its jar. Times were hard. Dripping hardly stained the bread, these days. 'I know!' she said suddenly. 'It's someone selling to the Indians!'

The lawman went upstairs, not speaking, and had a bath. He came down again. It was nearly noon.

'There's a thought,' he said.

He knew Indians and Indian territory like the back of his hand. He had known it in the days when it was Ye Olde Kopper Kettle. He took his helmet off, and went in. His serge arm rasped on the flock wallpaper, and an Indian slid out of nowhere at the sound.

'I am saying good day to you, what incredibly magnificent weather we are having, my goodness,' said the lawman, who had studied their ways and knew their tongues. 'Is it possible for you to be telling me what it is you are offering on the Businessman's Special this fine day?'

'Lamb curry,' grunted the Indian, 'tandoori chicken, mutton Madras.'

'Would it be possible for you to be giving me the incredibly necessary information concerning where you are purchasing this meat, by Jove?' said the lawman.

'Bloke comes Wednesdays,' said the Indian. 'Does me first, then he's off down the OK Grill-Room, isn't he? Probably catch him there now, if you're quick.'

'It has been an indescribable pleasure talking to you, oh my word, yes,' said the lawman, and backed out, bowing.

The sun glared fierce in the street. It hung overhead, like a great brass gong. It was noon. There was no-one else about. He thought of getting the Doc, but this was the time he took his linctus. He thought of asking some of the other citizens, but he knew what their reaction would be. They'd tell him to do something.

He was about to tiptoe, with his slow, easy, loping tiptoe, past the OK Grill-Room, when the door opened, and a man came out. He wore a black jacket, waistcoat and striped trousers, and a bowler hat. In one hand he carried an umbrella, in the other a rifle. He looked at the lawman.

'Oh I say!' he said. 'Haw, haw, haw! Well I jolly old never! A jolly old harry coppers!'

The lawman looked at the gun, and he looked at the man, and his throat was dry. But a man had to do what a man had to do. The lawman jerked his head towards a Jaguar parked at the kerb. A sheep's head was sticking out of the boot, dripping on the pullets tied to the rear bumper.

'Is this your car?' said the lawman.

'Jolly old is, I'm afraid, haw, haw, haw!' said the man with the gun.

The lawman drew in his breath.

'Can't leave it there,' he said. 'That's a double yellow line.'

This excerpt from 'Golfing For Cats' by Alan Coren (Robson Books Ltd.) was first published in Punch magazine.

"Now, Mrs Abthorpe, if you think you see the man who assaulted you, we just want you to touch him on the shoulder."

"No, I didn't recognise any of those men."

First appeared in Private Eye

Court Circular

John Smith admitted striking the police officer with a five foot iron bar. "I was just throwing the bar away in case someone tumbled on it when PC. Spink got in the way." He said.
Howdenshire Gazette.

One of the two men who took a JCB mechanical digger from a police sports ground in Widemarsh St. to give to a friend "as an engagement present" appeared for sentence on Wednesday.
Hereford Times

"I find streaking morally wrong" he continued "If the good Lord had intended us to run around with no clothes on then I am sure we would all have been born stark naked".
Kidderminster Observer

When a police constable asked Michael Maloney why he had 22 packets of ham under his jacket, the Irishman told him it was for sandwiches. His mate, he added, was just buying an onion and some bread to go with it. But the constable did not believe him.
Southern Evening Echo.

A man who was arrested in Sutton Coldfield for being drunk and disorderly told the police his name was Enid Blyton. Not until he was put in a cell did they realise he was not the famous authoress of childrens stories, Sutton magistrates were told last Thursday.
Sutton Coldfield News

Millworker Graham Lindley, aged 24, who broke into gas and electricity meters, told police: "I was out of work and didn't go to the dole because I don't believe in it. I don't think it is right to have money without working for it."
Manchester Evening Post

A man accused of being a Peeping Tom told police who found him that he was looking for a chiropodist to cure his athletes foot.
Hemel Hempstead Echo

Miss Taylor of Trowbridge, had the four tyres of her Triumph Herald car maliciously slashed when parked outside her house. Police say that a sharp instrument must have been used.
Wiltshire Times & News

Koay Siew Soon, an undertaker, was fined £5 in Malaysia when he admitted trespassing into a hospital and selling coffins to live patients.
Bristol Evening Post

EV'NIN ALL

The late Supreme Court Justice Oliver Wendell Holmes was once asked for advice from a young lawyer. "If you're strong on the law and weak on the facts", said Justice Holmes, "elaborate on the law".

"What if I'm weak on both law and facts?" said the young lawyer.

"Then bang on the table".

"I don't think we can do much about it. He's playing the national anthem."

The defense and prosecution lawyer became embroiled in a name calling contest. The defense yelled, "You are a lowdown crook and so phony you couldn't get a job in a parrot's show".

"And you are a cheap shyster who can be bought by the worst criminal in the world", screamed the prosecution.

The judge banged his gavel. "That's enough. Now that the learned counsel have identified themselves, let us continue the case".

"Move it!"

The long-winded lawyer droned until the judge gave a meaningful yawn, "I trust, Your Honor", said the lawyer, "that I'm not engaging in a trespass on the important time of the noble court".

"There is a difference", the judge solemnly noted, "between trespassing on time and encroaching on eternity".

"We're looking for a hit-and-run white-liner!"

A young police cadet was asked, "If you were alone in a police car and being pursued by a gang of bank robbers at seventy miles per hour, what would you do?"

"Eighty", he replied.

The Daily Blooper

SILENT SINGER

NEGRO singer Gererod Dorsetta has refused to give any evidence to New York police about the night club shooting which resulted in Billy Daniels, the coloured singer, being charged with assault and carrying a gnu.

Daily Mail

After you have switched off you are now ready to connect up the four wires. But don't try to connect the wife between A and B or you may get a shock.

Electrical paper

BABY SHOW

Best Baby under Six Months; Best Baby under Twelve Months; Best Baby under Two Years; Best Baby under Three Years.

Rules for Exhibitors:— All Exhibits become the property of the Committee as soon as staged, and will be sold for the benefit of the Hospital at the termination of the exhibition.

Exhibition programme

MAGISTRATES WERE IMPRESSED

SALISBURY magistrates gave a Bulford man a conditional discharge when he appeared on a theft charge because they were impressed by the way he was trying to help himself.

Southern Evening Echo

A PAPER published a heading, "Half the Council are crooks". It was asked to retract it, so it published the heading, "Half the Council are Not Crooks".

Lloyd Memorial Home

And when policewomen with the raiding party searched the woman who rented the house they found £32 in notes hidden in her brassiere.

The money, said Mr. John Culpin, prosecuting at Bedford, was part of a treasure chest the woman and her sister had built up.

Tired of appearing in westerns, the film star said he wanted to try more dramatic or romantic *rolls;* something he could get his teeth into.

—FALMOUTH (ORE.) ADVOCATE

The Queen and President Nixon exchanged gifts of silver-framed photographs during the President's visit to Britain. The Queen's gift was of two coloured autographed photographs of herself and Prince Philip, and the President's gift was a coloured autographed photograph of himself.

The woman, of excellent previous character, was bound over for three years on charges of stealing by finding.

Dublin Evening Press

School cuts out the human biology

Four pages have been cut out of all copies of a biology textbook used by a class of 11 to 12-year-olds in a Cardiff secondary school. The pages deal with human reproduction. The headmaster of Ty Celyn Secondary, Mr A. S. J. Heale, said: "I don't want to discuss it. It is an internal matter."

Sunday Times

Mounting problems for young couples

Mr. Root said that although there might be evidence of premarital intercourse by young people there was little to suggest that this pattern persisted after marriage.

The Western Gazette

Celebrating his 35th wedding anni versary he claimed he had proven his devotion to his wife by the fact that he had never left his wife alone a single night since they had been married.

—BRATON (IOWA) NEWS

GOVERNMENT TO ACT ON PIRATE RADIO STATIONS

BILL PROMISED BY BENN

DAILY TELEGRAPH REPORTER

Rugby—Metropolitan Police 7, Wasps 15

Wasps impressive in mud

THEM & US

"Other people have to pay taxes, as well, Mr. Yeatman, so would you please spare us the dramatics".

There are, of course, far too many of Them and not nearly enough of Us — and what's more, They are out to stop Us from doing or getting almost everything we want, let alone going where we like.

It is, for instance, They who devised the fiendish process of applying for a passport — They, indeed, who invented the passport itself. And the thing I mind most about **that** *(apart from having to have the wretched thing at all) is that having gone through the bother of looking up date of birth, number of feet, colour of eyeballs, there's only a miserable little half-line for "special peculiarities", and if there's one thing I want to let myself go on, it's that. I don't need half a line, I want a whole page to explain my peculiar and unique self — how sensitive I am to noise, nosey Customs officials, transistor radios, flies on the food and bugs in the bedroom. And that's only for starters.*

And another thing — I don't see why I should have to have a thing called an **Annual Certificate of Compliance** *pasted inside the back cover of my passport. Apart from the fact that I'm not in the habit of issuing certificates of anything addressed to anyone, I'm not having every little representative of Them with the right to rifle through my passport getting the idea that it also gives him the right to rifle through* **me.**

Now an **Annual Certificate of Defiance** *might be different.*

K.B.

THE NEW IMMORALITY

by ALAN COREN

ACROSS THE TINY, fetid expanse of Magoon, latest of Africa's independent republics, the monsoon gouted down, green and gloomy. The six thousand inhabitants, to avoid going mad from the incessant plopping of raindrops on the mbona leaves, had all retired to their holes to watch *Batman,* and the only movement on the surface of the saturated territory was the sluggish drift of a dugout punt, circling aimlessly on the ornamental lake in front of the Houses of Parliament. Or, more accurately in front of where the Houses of Parliament had stood until the day before, when the Loyal Magoon Opposition had kicked them down in a fit of pique.

In consequence, the punt was now the pro tem home of the Magoon Cabinet: they sat, wretched, with the oily rain streaming down their Gannex macs (an Independence gift from London), pondering the latest stumbling-block to Magoon's chances at the top tables of the world. Due to it's unique geographical position at the crossroads of Africa, the Gross National Product of Magoon consisted of tolls levied against neighbouring heads of state who wished to cross Magoon in order to see how other states were getting on, either to subvert them, or to offer them their professional services. This also meant that a national defence system was unnecessary, since everyone needed Magoon as a buffer state, and could not take the risk of occupying it.

Yet, while Magoon seemed to enjoy a Utopian situation, wooed by everyone, coveted by no-one, and self-sufficient without the irritation of having to produce anything, all was not well. As the PM was constantly telling his flock, economic sufficiency was not enough: as a lifelong fan of *Readers Digest* and anything else he could pinch, he entertained shimmering visions of transforming Magoon into a torch of tolerance and progressive thought by whose glow the whole world might be illuminated. He saw himself as the Father Of His People, a truth which seventy per cent of the female population stood ready to endorse, and had done much to introduce such enlightened legislation as the Cabinet Ministers' Droit de Seigneur Act (1966) and the Official Ordinance maintaining the Divine Right of Prime Ministers in perpetua.

But still the old-age rigid moral structure of Magoon stood in his way: until the people could be persuaded to relax the moral code that made them a laughing-stock throughout the civilised world, Magoon's dream of becoming the pilot of the world's enlightenment would remain just that. It was to this end that the PM had convened the extraordinary Cabinet meeting that currently stared gloomily from the gunwales of the punt at the pitted surface of the lake.

"Bleeding cesspool of Victorian puritanism," said the PM at last, "that's what we are. A Mockery of Freethinking. I was reading in *The Times* where even the British Church refuses to condemn extra-marital sexual intercourse out of hand. And look at us!"

The Cabinet stared at him from their sodden cushions. As the PM was the only Magoonian allowed to read outside papers, the news left them somewhat uncertain. The Minister of Finance cleared his throat.

"What's sexual intercourse?" he said.

The PM looked at him bitterly.

"You're an ignorant sod, Ngaga," he said. "No idea what goes on outside, have you? It's making love.

The Cabinet frowned, puzzled.

"They only just started making love in Britain, then?" asked one.

"Of course not!" snapped the PM. "But British society expects it to be confined to married couples."

The punt suddenly rocked with wild laughter. Swans flew up from the lake in fear, and, on the bank, the watching baboons barked.

"Pull this one," cried the Chancellor of the Exchequer, wiping his eyes, "it's got bells on!"

"I swear it," said the PM. "They can only do it after going through some recognised form of official ceremony."

"I never heard such a load of old rubbish," said the Minister of Transport. "Next thing, you'll tell us they just do it to have kids."

"More or less," said the Prime Minister.

The Cabinet snorted, and spat, and stamped their naked feet.

"And you call *them* enlightened," said the Chancellor.

"They're changing," said the PM. Then he paused, watching them. Slowly he smiled. "In England," he said, "there's no such sin as eating."

The Cabinet gasped.

"It's true," said the PM. "There's no set times, no rules, no secrecy, nothing. *Men and women actually eat together—"*

"They'd see one another's mouths" shrieked the Chief Whip.

"—even children. They don't eat alone, in cupboards, like us. They even eat *in public!* In large groups."

"It's disgusting!" cried the Cabinet. "It's vile!"

The PM leaned forward, grinning.

"They even eat because they *enjoy* it!" he whispered. "Not just to keep alive. Not just to satisfy a biological function."

The Cabinet sat stunned. But, after a moment or two, they began to glance at one another, tentatively. The PM sighed heavily.

"You don't have to look like that," he said. "I know what you lot get up to when the lights are out. Nice square meal in the cupboard at home, all a man could want, you still can't resist nipping round the corner for a bit of how's-your-father with the odd ham sandwich, can you? Or a nice piece of fatty wart-hog. Or a peanut."

The Chancellor shrugged.

"It goes on," he said. "We're only human."

"Exactly," said the PM. "What I want to do is bring it all out into the open. A new Morality. Put Magoon in the forefront of civilisation, see? Let My People Eat. Have State-licensed restaurants, the lot: look how much better that'd be than having our teenagers crawling off to dark alleys for a quick yam, never knowing what they might pick up. We'd have government services helping people having trouble with their eating lives. Have clinics, too. These days, half the country has indigestion, only they're too terrified of the social stigma to go to a doctor. They can cure it now, you know. Food Without Shame, lads, that's our motto."

They had listened, awestruck, and now, like intelligent employees the world over, they cheered their leader to the echo, and, singing a hitherto forbidden shanty about a woman who could never get enough boiled cabbage, they struck out for the sodden shore.

During the next few weeks, controversy raged. The Opposition claimed that the Government was in the pay of the greengrocers, the Magoonian national broadsheet was filled with stories of incontinent flaming youth who'd scoffed themselves into early graves, and much was made of the Undermining Of Civilisation As We Know It. Yet open controversy is itself a kind of freedom, and before long, facts hitherto ignored or suppressed began to surface. Statistics emerged: sixty per cent of Magoonians had never really experienced true intestinal satisfaction, thirty per cent confessed to having had at least one illicit meal, twenty per cent wanted to allow communal eating between consenting adults, and half the country was prepared to compromise by eating with the lights on. Pundits appeared, and waxed rich, men who wanted eating habits taught in the schools, who wanted food shown in the cinema, who wanted eating clubs established. Tales were told of vile eating orgies in the hills, where couples swopped packets of sandwiches, of evil old Magoonians who pressed boiled sweets into little girls' hands and hung about on streetcorners exposing individual pork pies. A noted Magoonian intellectual appeared on TV and shouted "Eat off!" during a debate on the Irish Question. And, bit by inevitable bit, permissiveness extended until the people thought about nothing but food and whether they were getting as much of it as the next man and if they were really enjoying it at all and if too much of it made your hair fall out. Books appeared with titles like *Eating Problems At 45* and *Is Heavy Chewing A Sin?* and soon everyone was more worried about food and the eating of it than they had ever been before. Magazines sprang up, with glossy gatefolds of cod and chips and columns of advice to those without teeth, and Magoon was suddenly filled with seedy frankfurter joints and egg clubs. And lust piled upon lust, and neurosis upon neurosis, and doubt upon doubt, until, very, very late in the day, the Church of Magoon at last came out with its definitive statement:

THE GREAT TOAD SAYS
EATING'S ALL RIGHT

But by then nobody had any appetite left at all.

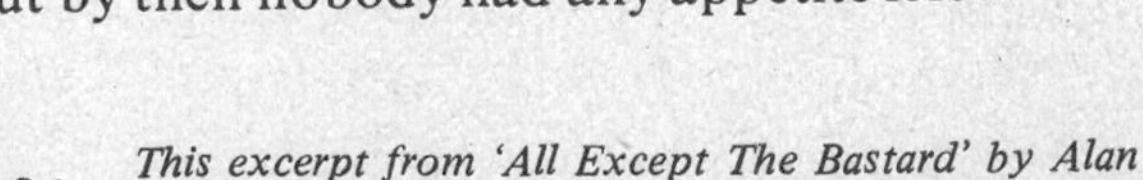
This excerpt from 'All Except The Bastard' by Alan Coren (Robson Books Ltd.) was first published in Punch magazine.

As part of a campaign to publicise the position of American Indians, a Cherokee arrived for a convention in New York dressed in full Indian costume.

He decided to book in at a very exclusive hotel. The clerk looked at him doubtfully, but finally handed him a registration card.

"Just put your X on the top line."

The Indian carefully marked an X; then put another X alongside.

"What's the other X for?" the clerk demanded.

"That's my PhD from Harvard."

In one of the circles of hell is a deep swamp to which liars are dispatched after death. The bigger the liar, the deeper he sinks into the mire.

Hitler and Goering are in it up to their chins. They glare, full of envy, at Goebbels, who is only up to his belly.

"You're a bigger liar than the rest of us put together," screams Hitler. "You invented the Big Lie technique! How come you haven't sunk down as deep as us two?"

"I'm standing on Stalin's shoulders," says Goebbels.

"Amin is a fool!" shouted a worker, after a few drinks.

He was arrested and sent for trial. His sentence ran as follows:

"Three months' imprisonment for vilifying the head of state. Ten years' hard labour for betraying state secrets."

YOU CAN'T WITHDRAW LIKE THIS! ... YOU HAVE A RESPONSIBILITY TO MANKIND!

WE MUST BUILD SOCIETIES, AND ESTABLISH COMMERCE, AND CREATE POLITICAL PHILOSOPHIES, AND ECONOMIC DIVERSION-

SO WE CAN COMPETE, AND CHALLENGE, AND BUILD-UP ARMS AGAINST ONE ANOTHE.....✱....

HOW LONG DOES IT TAKE TO GROW A BEARD LIKE THAT ?

Repression doesn't kill humour – it just drives it underground!
Here's a selection of political jokes mostly from the Big Red Joke Book.

REAL POLITIK?

One afternoon, Brezhnev disguised his appearance and went to see a film in a Moscow suburban cinema. After the feature film there was a short news-reel.

A picture of Brezhnev appeared on the screen. Everyone stood up, except for Brezhnev himself. He sat there with tears in his eyes, deeply moved by this spontaneous show of popular affection.

A man tapped him on the shoulder and whispered: "Get up, you fool! We all think like you do, but what's the point of putting your head in a noose?"

Alexander the Great, Julius Caesar and Napoleon were watching the October Parade in Moscow's Red Square.

Alexander could scarcely take his eyes off the tanks. "If I had had chariots like these," he said, "I could have conquered the whole of Asia."

Caesar admired the intercontinental ballistic missiles.

"If I had had such arrows," he declared, "I could have ruled the world."

Napoleon glanced up from the copy of *Pravda* he was reading.

"And if I had had a newspaper like this," he exclaimed, "no-one would even have heard of Waterloo."

The Shah of Iran was having trouble keeping his workers in line, so he thought he might invest in a few dozen extra tanks. Consequently he visited an arms factory in Coventry.

He had just met the managing director when the lunchtime hooter sounded. To the Shah's horror, hundreds of workers downed tools and rushed out of the factory.

"We must escape!" cried the Shah. "The workers have risen. We will have to capture one of your tanks and fight our way to safety."

"It's nothing to worry about," the managing director assured him. "It happens every day. In half an hour's time, another hooter will sound and they'll all rush back in again."

"Really?" the Shah replied. "In that case, forget the tanks — I'll take a thousand hooters instead."

MOSCOW jokes department — here is the latest going the rounds in Yugoslavia: A delegation from Belgrade found themselves queuing endlessly for food, until in exasperation they agreed one of them should be deputed to take the ultimate revenge and shoot Leonid Brezhnev. Within half an hour the chosen one returned red-faced to the congratulations of his colleagues, only to admit 'I didn't do it, the queue was too long.'

Carter and Brezhnev were chatting over the hot line one morning when the Soviet leader said:

"By the way, Jimmy, I had a dream about Washington last night. I dreamed I saw the White House, and as I watched, the Stars and Stripes was lowered and in its place flew a big Red Flag."

"Oh really?" replied Carter, not amused. "Well I had a dream last night too, Leonid. I was standing in Red Square looking at the Kremlin, and there over the top flew a big red banner with writing on it."

"There's nothing unusual in that," said Brezhnev, pleased to have got one over on Carter. "By the way, what did the writing say?"

"I don't know, Leonid. I can't read Chinese."

A Russian and a Chinese are discussing the idea of peaceful co-existence. According to the Russian, it is entirely possible for capitalism and socialism to live peacefully side by side. The Chinese vehemently disputes this.

In order to prove his point, the Russian takes him to Moscow zoo, where a lamb and a wolf are kept together in the same cage.

"Just as the lamb and the wolf lie down together," said the Russian, "so two opposed social systems can live peacefully on the same planet."

The Chinese is deeply impressed.

"But how on earth do you manage it?" he asks. "A wolf and a lamb in the same cage!"

"It's simply a question of organisation," answers the Russian. "We put a new lamb in each morning."

Q. Why do Roumanian policeman always go around in threes?

A. It's official policy. They always send out one who can read, one who knows how to make telephone calls and one to keep an eye on the two dangerous intellectuals.

Before leaving on a trade mission to Bulgaria, one of the delegates took the trouble to learn enough of the language to make a short speech at one of the dinners held for the delegation in Sofia. As he rose to his feet however, he realised that he'd forgotten the Bulgarian for "Ladies and Gentlemen". Glancing frantically round, he spotted two rather obvious doors in a corner of the dining room — and clearing his throat, he began his speech. It was received with mystified smiles but not much enthusiasm. Sitting down, he asked his neighbour how he thought the speech had gone down. "Not badly, comrade, but in Bulgaria we usually start our speeches with the words 'Ladies and Gentlemen' and not 'Water Closets and Urinals'.

IN KAMPALA

An Asian was found guilty of a petty offence, and was sentenced to walk around carrying a sign which said 'Asians out, Amin in'.

The police kept a lookout to make sure he was doing his punishment, but they couldn't find him in any of the streets. Finally, they tracked him down. He was walking round and round the local cemetery.

☆

Security guard in a Uganda concentration camp calls over a prisoner.

"You there! Come here. Now listen carefully: "I've got a glass-eye. I want you to tell me which one it is. If you guess right, nothing will happen to you. If you guess wrong, I'll shoot you on the spot. Which one is it?"

"The left one, Mr. Kommandant."

"How the hell did you guess?"

"It's got such a kind look about it."

★

One passenger in an overcrowded Kampala bus tapped another on the shoulder:

"Excuse me, are you a member of the armed forces?"

"No."

"Is your father or anyone else in your family a member of the armed forces?"

"No."

"Are you a police officer, perhaps?"

"No."

"And your family?"

"My family have nothing whatsoever to do with the police," said the man, getting irritated.

"You're sure you're not a secret policeman?"

"No! Now for God's sake stop pestering me with your questions!"

"In that case, would you mind getting off my foot?"

☆

IN CAIRO

After the Six-Day War, two Arabs were gloomily discussing the disastrous showing of the Arab armies:

"Why do you think we did so badly? Was it because the Russian weapons were no good?"

"The weapons were fine. It was the Russian military textbooks that let us down."

"What did they say?"

"'First retreat and draw the enemy into your own territory. Then wait for the winter snows . . .'"

An American and a Russian got into an argument about the meaning of the words 'freedom of speech'.

"Let me give you an example," said the American. "Suppose I sit down and write a letter to the White House saying that the President of the United States is an idiot, nothing at all will happen to me."

"What's so wonderful about that? If I sit down and write a letter to the Kremlin saying that the President of the United States is an idiot, they'll make me a Hero of the Soviet Union."

Kovacs went to the police in Budapest and asked for a passport and permission to emigrate.

"And where do you want to emigrate to, Mr. Kovacs?" asked the police superintendant.

"Holland."

"Aren't you happy in Budapest?"

"I can't grumble."

"Don't you have a good job here?"

"Can't grumble."

"Don't you have a pleasant enough life?"

"Can't grumble."

"In that case, why do you want to emigrate to Holland?"

"Because there I *can* grumble."

A Russian and an English businessman were talking.

"What are your impressions of British industry?" asked one of the factory's directors.

"You still have much to learn," answered one of the Russians. "You should study our experience. In our country we work hard. We do not have tea-breaks every morning and every afternoon. We do not have strikes and go-slows. Demarcation disputes are unheard of in the Soviet Union. Each Soviet worker gives of his best, and would never think of pursuing his own private interests at the expense of the state."

"It's clear from what you say," replied the director, "that you don't have any Communists in your factories to cause trouble."

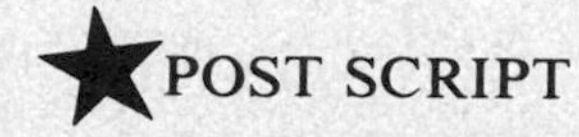

POST SCRIPT

"*Pravda* is going to hold a competition for the best political joke."

"What's the first prize?"

"Twenty years."

'The Big Red Joke Book' published by Pluto Press

from the Calman Gallery.

If we can now phone Shanghai – we should soon be able to get through to Holborn again...

OUT OF ORDER

I dont mind who knows about my bank balance as long as they don't tell me

CON CALLS TO BANKS

Silence is more golden than ever...

POST DEARER

At least in the old days you could always put your head in the gas oven...

STRIKES! GAS OFF FOOD UP

COLD PILLS

All I've ever been offered is luncheon vouchers...

SCANDAL – BRIBES, SEX PARTIES

TAX-FREE PAYMENTS

I hope it doesn't get wet and shrink even further

POUND FLOATS

And still got no sense

MAN 2¼ MILLION YEARS OLD

NIXON WINS

Calman Cartoons from 'My God' & 'This Pestered Isle' published by Souvenir Press Ltd.

Web of Intrigue

I WAS NOT unduly disturbed by Mr. Iain Sproat's allegation that the Government had been infiltrated by a desperate band of Communists, Marxists, Trotskyites and similar cut-throats, all trudging about the Commons with snow on their boots, plotting to deliver the country into the hands of the Soviet Union.

Quite frankly I don't think there's anything to worry about because, if any commonsense still exists in the Kremlin, the Soviet Union wouldn't have us as a gift. Six months with Britain as a dependent satellite and Russia's economy would be in as rotten a state as ours and it would be touch and go which of us was first in the queue outside the IMF waiting for a handout.

Besides, even if what Mr. Sproat says is true, there's clearly nothing we can do about it because, according to Mr. Andrew Faulds, the only viable alternative to the mob of thinly-disguised Commissars currently manipulating the Cabinet is fractionally worse, the main opposition party consisting apparently of demented Fascists who regard Attila the Hun as having been somewhat to the left of Lenin.

"I am prepared," said Mr. Faulds, "to give the house now twelve names of Conservative MPs whose allegiances I very much question in the context of their connection with the Right wing."

He didn't actually go so far as to say who they were but I wait expectantly to learn that Mrs. Thatcher is really Eva Braun with a facelift, that Martin Bormann didn't go to the Argentine at all, but is alive and well in Westminster and calling himself Ted Heath, and, for good measure, that Enoch Powell bought his moustache second-hand from Hitler during the Nazi Government's clearance sale just before it went into liquidation in 1945.

Goodness knows into whose hands this lot is planning to deliver us, but I shouldn't be at all surprised if it was Chile's.

Meanwhile, a far more alarming revelation, one that in a less phlegmatic nation might have caused panic in the streets — and did indeed cause me to panic in the streets when I read of it — was that there exists in this country a species of spider which is *six inches* long. It hasn't been seen about much lately, and thank God for that, but when it does make a public appearance it tends to do so in Suffolk.

It's known as a giant raft spider and, even by the most unbiased accounts, is a frightful-looking object, having thick fleshy legs and a brown body with orange stripes. Nature conservancy groups think it may have fallen victim to the drought and I just pray that they're right. If you want my opinion the only good spider is an extinct spider.

What terrifies me, though, is that I once spent a holiday in Suffolk and might quite easily have encountered a gang of these monsters darting in and out of the undergrowth (such being their obnoxious habit) in search of victims, and then what would I have done?

Well, actually, I know what I would have done. I would have done exactly what I did some years ago when, just as I was about to clean my teeth, I encountered a giant bath spider, easily an inch long, charging towards me with its fists clenched.

On that occasion, reacting with the uncanny swiftness for which I'm rightly renowned, I thrust my wife between me and it and ran out of the room, slamming the door behind me. And I don't mind admitting that I'd have done precisely the same—only rather more quickly—if it had been a giant raft spider instead. Mind you, I expect I should have been sorry later after the spider had kicked the door down and lurched belching out of the house and I'd found the body of my wife, bones picked clean, on the bathroom floor but in such emergencies it's a case of sauve qui peut.

For make no mistake about it, no matter how strenuously the nature conservancy people try to convince us that giant raft spiders are harmless and live on insects, they can't kid me. No spider gets to be six inches long on a diet of flies, mate.

Why do you suppose rural Suffolk is so under-populated, eh? Why do you imagine that the nature groups which, for reasons unfathomable to me, want to try to preserve this species (in the unlucky event that some still survive) by digging trenches for them in the fens, have openly admitted that it's dangerous work?

I'll tell you why. It's because they know as well as I do that a giant raft spider wouldn't bother to sink its teeth into any insect smaller than a sheep and in fact lurks about the fens waiting to pounce on drunken peasants and well-meaning fools who turn up with spades and start digging trenches.

The thing that really worries me is that these creatures haven't been seen in Suffolk lately not because they're extinct but because they're on the move. Any day now they'll be sighted swaggering mob-handed down the London road in their brown and orange football jerseys. And then it won't matter if the country is run by Commies or Nazis because they'll be eaten along with the rest of us. Giant raft spiders rule, OK?

BARRY NORMAN – Guardian – 24. 11. 76

The perfect civil servant is the man who has a valid objection to any possible solution.

A Permanent Parliamentary Secretary, touring Devon in a car, lost his way and inquired of a stalwart Devonian: "Where am I?" "You are in a car", replied the local. The P.P.s. observed: "That is the perfect answer to a Parliamentary question. It is short, it is true and it does not add one iota to what is known already".

Public Works

An attempt was made to make use of an electronic machine to translate English into Russian. The phrase "Out of sight, out of mind" was fed into the machine. The answer came out in Russian and this was fed back into the machine to be translated into English. The answer came out: "Invisible idiot".

Evening Standard, Dec. 11, '75

Jak's new collection of cartoons from the Standard, I'm Oil Right, Jak, is available from newsagents and bookstalls, at 45p. Or from the Evening Standard by post 59p.

"It's not another siege—I've just been delivering the new telephone bills!"

London Express Service.

TAXING THE BRAIN

Keith Waterhouse asks...

My little daughter will be needing a pair of new sandals in April. Will I have to pay Value Added Tax on them?

Not if she eats them in the shop. If she only nibbles at one of the buckles while the shop assistant is trying to make sense of Customs and Excise Notice No. 700, you will have to pay VAT on the unconsumed portion of the sandals.

She is also fond of playing 'Pass the Parcel' at her birthday parties. Does the lucky child who finishes up with the parcel have to pay VAT on it?

Are you joking? EVERYBODY has to pay VAT on the parcel. As each child passes the parcel to the next, it must fill out an input and output voucher and add 10 per cent. However, the last child deducts the output from the input so, technically, nobody pays anything.

What's the big idea, then?

I'm not quite sure. I think 'Pass the Parcel' must be popular in Government circles, too.

Can you explain the difference between output and input in words of one syllable?

That's a pretty fat-headed question, isn't it? Obviously, output is what you pay out and input is what you rake in. No, hang about, though, I'm a liar. It's the other way round. You learn something new every day, don't you?

I am a brewer in a small way and I have a rat in my vat. If I buy a cat to get rid of the rat, will I have to pay VAT?

What on—the cat or the rat? As far as the rat is concerned, it would seem to be nibbling into your output so you can charge it as input. But the rat must provide you with an invoice.

As for the cat, it if eats the rat in the vat, your input will be decreased so you will have to pay VAT on the cat, which becomes output. If the rat eats the cat, your input will have consumed your output so you can claim back the VAT on the cat.

Will I be liable for Value Added Tax on the expense of burying my grandfather?

That depends on whether he is dead or not. If you are burying him just for fun, it becomes entertainment and you must pay VAT at every stage of the enterprise.

However, if your grandfather is actually deceased, and he is turning over in his grave at all this nonsense, and such a turnover exceeds £5,000 he must register immediately for VAT, unless, that is to say . . .

See here, Waterhouse, you haven't the faintest idea what you're talking about, have you?

Not really. Still, I bet I know as much about it as anyone else.

Excerpt from 'Mondays, Thursdays' published by Michael Joseph Ltd.

"We can do without your down to earth realism, Henshaw"

sendin' de cure damquick

Dear Bwana Prime Minister,

Re: NHS, British GPO, Kenya Medical Association, also de British Airways European an Overseas Division.

Fust let me say how pleased is dis subjeck on de agreement you done reach wid de Liberals. Willy de husban saying effen we getting one more election or referendum, de Ndege family goin home. As de Kenyan livin in de GB I also don' get no satisfaction wid de NHS, de KMA, de British GPO, de British Airways in either division. Wid de achin' bonce, swole eyes an de spots all over de damn place, I writin my witchdoctah GP Doctah Ogola on Mount Kenya, for sendin de cure damquick.

Dr Ogola explainin' he no can send de oafs tro' de post no mo' as he sendin de Elephants earwax wid de Hyrax skin and de doin's from de Hyena, but de GPO here raisin' de terrible shauri wid de patient, my sister Mrs Kamau. Dr Ogola also gettin de snotty letter from de Customs an Exercise about pollutin de post.

Mrs Kamau an me we get de friend to take dis prescription by dhow to Dubai where it getting put on board de Conkorde. What a shauri is erruptin' wid de British Airways all divisions. De officials dey is runnin round and round de Conkorde sayin' wot de hell dis not a bloody prescription carrier it a supersonic service.

Mrs Kamau, she got de dengue fever an she sayin' "I want my prescription fust an yo no movin' nothin yo hear!" De officials bawlin "where in blazes dis prescription yo on about den madam?" Evalina quickly explainin "we sent fo de number one cure from Doctah Ogola on de Conkorde wot you tink? An stop pushin' me in de back so rough or I am also sendin' for de spot of Evil Eye." When de officials findin' de oafs on de Conkorde, de one small fellow he faint an everybody shoutin' at Mrs Kamau and Evalina.

So Willy de husban he done takin' me to de european doctah in de village, who doan roll de bones nor keepin de deafmask, but at least he makin wit de diagnostics. "Mrs Ndege" he says, "yo got de heavy allergy to de climate I feah, along wide de dandruff." "Waugh doctah!" shout Willy wid de fright, "dis ting be terminal den?" De doctah assurin de husband it goin to be qwite OK wid treatment wid de needle in de bum, but kweli! it sure bring de water to de eye.

"Doctah" I says, "de climate yo got not too hot an for one small island yo got maningi rain. I tink de Mungu in de sky got de needle wid de chronic economic crisis yo gottin."

Maybe you should suggest to de Gumment to send Dr Kimathi de witchdoctoh specialist from Mount Meru, a invitation. If he make suitable dawa in the Treasury wid de damu from de bats, mixed wid de soot, feathers from a Ostrich an a Black Mamba, yo gittin sorted.

Las' week I groanin wid de pain in de neck. "Doctah!" I cryin "de needle in de bum shiftin de achin' from de bonce to de neck. How long we goin wait for de pain to drop out from de feet den?" De doctah makin further searches all over de Evalina and sendin me to de white fella specialist in Hartley street, who snappin," git yo close orf Mrs Ndege," an he hittin me on de knee wid de rubber item lookin jus like de hammer. De scream I am makin send Willy in clear tro' de curtain.

"Doctah! Wot goin on here man" he shoutin, "de pain not gittin to de knee yet, it still stuck in de neck!" De specialist rollin de eyes an lookin mighty fed up. "Mrs Ndege" he sayin "dere be notin' wrong wit yo on de body, it all in yo mind." Dist mos' niggling news. "Willy," I askin, "why you done tell me all dese europeans makin specialists when dey study at de London School ob Economics hey? Our doctah Ogola, he jus an ordinary GP witchdoctah, not even de specialist witchdoctah an he already knowin all de sickness startin in de mind, so wot up wid dis fella den?"

De specialist lookin like he done swallow de dungbeatle an he goin out an mutterin to de nurse, "get dese hypochondriacs out ob it nurse." De nurse pressin de bill in de han' at de door. "Wot dis Willy?" I ask de husban when I done see de fee which statin Twelve GNS. I tink they jus done nationalised de poun an dey askin for twelve Gumment Nationalised Subsidies. Where de hell we gettin dis new cash I wonder? Willy he sigh an he say "Doctah Ogola, he doin de diagnostics, de cure an supplying de medicine for seven East African shillings an de bottle ob Nubian gin."

Bwana Prime Minister, please to bring yo mighty influence to bear on de GPO an de British Airways mainly, fo gettin de oafs tro' de post or on de air freight, we not too fussy which. Also, kindly to have a word wid de Customs and Exercise who are gettin oppressive. Also de fellow doin all de nationalisation as he now busy wid de beer. Wot for I want to fill up de damlong buff form every time I askin for lager an lime in de pub man?

Kin' regards to de very sexy son in law yo gottin bwana.

Kwaheri sana,

Evalina Ndege (Mrs)

by EVELYN LITTLE

Snap!

RAC
P
FREE
PUBLIC
CONVENIENCES

VIEWS OF THE WORLD

PENSIONER REFUSES BAIL

Shortly after refusing to pay 47p for the breakfast he had consumed in a Birmingham cafe, Mr Francis Whelan, an 86-year-old pensioner, was arrested.

The next day he refused to be released. "Anyone who has had to struggle along on a pension would be mad to leave Winson Green Prison," he said. "It's a real treat. Three square meals a day, central heating and plenty of new faces."

Mr Whelan rejected bail and remained in prison for three months.

"His is a unique case," said Mr Sime, the Recorder, "in all my experience I have never heard of the prosecution applying for bail on the part of the accused."

"I was hoping to stay in for Christmas," Mr Whelan said. "They say it's very, very good. Unfortunately I'll just have to find a room somewhere."

Mr Whelan's incarceration cost nearly £400.

"Why should I worry about the taxpayer?" he said. "I fought in two wars and worked all my life. If I'm not a taxpayer, who is?"

Mr Whelan was described by a Social Worker as "both rational and intelligent."

Husband Impresses Wife At Work

On the day before her divorce Mrs Ursula Becker of Dortmund called at her husband's office to discuss the settlement of their property. In the course of her visit Mr Becker argued against their action, but in vain.

However, when the judge asked her to tell the court how long it had been since they made love, Mrs Becker was surprised to hear her husband shout: "It's a lie!" when she said: "At least 18 months ago."

"We made love on the floor of my office yesterday morning!" said Mr Becker. "I marked her bum with the office date-stamp."

Mrs Becker's petition was denied.

Rowdies turn to Jelly

After the Prime Minister of Australia, one Mr McMahon, had been pelted with jelly-babies in the town of Perth, secret service agents collected the evidence, arrested fifteen assorted rowdies, and prior to charging them, returned to guard their leader while he addressed a crowd of several thousand voters.

When everyone had gone home they returned to base and released their catch.

"We could bring no charges," said a secret service spokesman, "because the evidence had been eaten by Bozo, a cockatoo."

Anxious Wife claims Husband is a Sucker

Finding that her husband liked sleeping with their baby's dummy in his mouth, an American wife asked him if he would like a bottle made up to go with it. He would, so she did, and thus they continued for several years. Eventually the wife became anxious; not, she assured the journalist to whom she wrote for advice, because either of them felt unhappy, but because her husband is a senior executive on the Apollo Programme.

Ceremony too much for Groom

Miss Naomi Nicely of Greensburg, Pennsylvania, has asked the Westmoreland Court to declare her to be an "official widow".

Miss Nicely and/or Mrs Neiderhiser was standing at the altar rails with Robert, her husband to be, when, in the middle (or, as she is claiming, "at the end") of the ceremony, he dropped dead.

Giving evidence on behalf of Miss Nicely, The Rev. Captain Rag of Fort Palmer Unitarian Mission, said: "Mr Neiderhiser fell to the floor as he uttered the binding words 'I do'. As I bent over him he whispered, 'My God — I do', whereupon he died. The ceremony was over."

JUVENILLE SNAKE BANNED

Senhor Michaelangeli Phuta of Belem, Brazil, was arrested for entering a cinema with Dolores, his pet Boa constrictor, around his neck. Senhor Kaukmann, manager of El Stella, Belem's only cinema, said: "The snake was under age".

Senhor Phuta said: "Dolores goes where I go. We had been looking forward to *Gone with the Wind* for six years."

VICAR PRAYS TO STOP TRAIN AT YORK

Travellers on the 3.20 express from Newcastle to London were surprised when, having assured a fellow passenger, Reverend Robert Middlemiss, that they would not be stopping at York, he fell onto his knees and began to pray for the train to slow down.

Their surprise turned to amazement when it did, and, after apologising to them for any inconvenience he might have caused, the Reverend Middlemiss opened the carriage door and jumped out.

"I was booked to address the British Sailor's Society in York," said Vicar Middlemiss, "I did not want to be late, I am a firm believer in the power of prayer."

A spokesman for British Rail said that Reverend Middlemiss had contravened a bye-law.

Chihuahua Pups For Sale

Mrs Joan Cooper, a dog-lover from Essex, offered her two Chihuahua pups for sale.

Telephoned by a prospective buyer, Mrs Cooper was asked, "Are they matching?"

"They are about the same size," she answered.

"But," said the customer, "are they the same colour?"

"Unfortunately not," said Mrs Cooper. "One is black and the other is cream."

"Ah," said the customer, "that won't do. We want to use them as bookends — after they have been killed and stuffed, of course."

Much of the material for the 'Views Of The World' was originally collected and published in Private Eye.

H-H-HANCOCK

There have been many attempts to describe Tony Hancock's kind of comedy and Hancock himself struggled to define it, never with much success.

Worth far more than any of them is a close look at a typical *Hancock's Half Hour* script as heard on radio. Like the one where he stood for Parliament.

It opens with Hancock, Miss Pugh (Hatti Jacques) and Bill Kerr sitting down for breakfast and Hancock demanding that he should be the one to open the new packet of cornflakes as he wants first chance at the little plastic soldier. It is a month in which the manufacturers are urging cornflake eaters to make up their own guards' band and Hancock needs a trumpet player to complete his set. He has already got six trombone players. Miss Pugh protests. She bought forty-three packets for him last month just to find the flute player.

'They'll never get eaten,' she complained.

'Yes they will,' says Hancock. 'The next party we have, put some salt on them and tell everybody they're crisps.'

Miss Pugh is scornful. When she buys cornflakes she buys them for the cornflakes not little plastic guardsmen.

A typical woman's attitude, says Hancock. No imagination. 'It's the thrill of the hunt,' he says. 'Getting your set together. Look at them up there on the mantelpiece. Marching along there. What a stirring sight. A complete band . . . minus a trumpet player.'

Then emotionally: 'I've been waiting three weeks for that trumpet player. Breakfast is making me a nervous wreck I don't mind telling you . . . '

Bill asks him for the trombone player and offers a drummer. Hancock refuses. Miss Pugh tells them to stop squabbling. 'Next week they'll probably finish with the guardsman and start an entirely different set.'

Hancock is indignant. 'Oh will they. Miss Pugh, take a letter to the makers. Dear Sir, I hereby warn you that if you dicontinue putting guardsmen in your cornflakes before I've got my set, I shall in future eat porridge. Yours sincerely, A. Hancock. Age seven and a half. There. That'll frighten them.'

Now he is ready for his bacon and pease pudding. Miss Pugh is already tucking into hers. 'Look at her plate piled up there. You can't see her, just her arms coming round the sides. Are you there?'

Bill Kerr is reading the paper and Hancock snatches it from him. 'By the time you've stumbled through it, it'll be yesterday's. Give us it here.'

He reads out bits. 'Hallo, I see he's got three years. I knew he was guilty when I saw his photo last week. He had a moustache. That was enough for me.'

There are long, audacious pauses between each item.

'Butter's going up in China . . . snow in the North of Scotland . . . Man denies weekend in caravan.'

He turns the page, 'Oh, she's nice . . . seventeen year old model from Gateshead . . . record crop of rice in Tibet this year . . . vicar punches driving instructor . . . she doesn't look seventeen, does she?'

The question about whether the beauty from Gateshead is seventeen or older becomes a running gag for the rest of the half hour. But there is another item—an election in East Cheam.

Hancock hasn't any time for politicians—they're all the same. 'I have nothing but the utmost dislike for politicians.'

Kerr's been thinking: 'If you break the end of the trombone, it'll look like a trumpet,' he says.

Hancock tells him to shut up.

Sid enters on his way after working all night. He puts down his sack in the corner. It clanks. Hancock looks into it. It's full of stolen metal. Sid offers to pay for his breakfast with two foot of waste pipe. Hancock orders him to take it off his table.

Sid assures him that it's worth seven and a tanner. Hancock is offended, stands on principle. 'You come in here trying to barter with your night's pickings, two foot of pipe for some cornflakes and pease pudding. Whatever next?

It's worth two curly bits and a section of guttering any time, that is.'

The deal is on.

Sid gets his cornflakes and asks where the little plastic guardsman is. He too needs a trumpet player. He knows a bloke in Epsom who's got six trumpet players and is after a trombone player.

'Stone me!' says Hancock. 'I've got a boxful of trombone players. It's the distribution that's all wrong.' He didn't have this trouble with his fag cards.

Sid is resigned. 'That's the way it goes. Anything in the papers?'

'No, nice bird from Gateshead on page two. Seventeen it says.'

Sid doesn't think she's seventeen either, reads about the price of Chinese butter, comments on a man sent to gaol for three years and says: 'I reckon this bird's nearer twenty-one, you know.'

They get back to politics via the paper's cartoon which they both admire, though they confess that they don't know what it means.

Hancock's profession is established. Saying the girl was seventeen might have been a printer's error.

'It does happen,' says Hancock. 'They called me Tommy Hitchcock the other week.'

He had written in demanding an apology. 'Look!' Sid reads: 'We apologise for any embarrassment caused last week when we wrote about Mr. Tommy Hitchcock. We were of course referring to that celebrated comedian Mr. Terry Hancick.'

'Well it's near enough,' said Hancock. 'You can't keep writing can you?'

They talk about the local M.P.'s application for the Chiltern Hundreds.

Hancock knows what it means. 'The Chiltern Hundreds,' he explains, 'is an ancient custom. They apply for it when they want promotion. They get a hundred pounds, a new suit, and a badge allowing them to use the House of Lords canteen without being accompanied by Black Rod. I think you'll find that's right.'

There is a knock at the door. Kenneth Williams is there with his 'good morning'. He asks Miss Pugh if she's Mrs. Hancock. 'Do you want a punch on the nose?' she replies.

He comes in and Hancock is identified as 'the fat one in the red nightshirt'. He thinks it is another seeker after food. 'I'm sorry, mush,' he says, 'there's no breakfast left.'

But the caller doesn't want breakfast. He is from the East Cheam Independents and they want Hancock to stand as their candidate in the forthcoming election. It doesn't matter that he knows nothing about politics. He has been on television, hasn't he? Well, that's all they demand of any candidate. Hancock's final shred of reluctance is swept away when he is told that he could even become Prime Minister.

'That'd be good. I could step out of an aeroplane waving me hat, couldn't I?'

Yes, he is told, and go straight through customs. This has an immediate appeal for Sid. 'Think of all those watches we could get through.'

Hancock agrees to stand.

As he is leaving, the caller spies the cornflake packet. 'You don't happen to have . . . ' he begins when Hancock interrupts: 'No, only four trombone players.'

To Hancock, the election is a mere formality. He feels very important. He quotes: 'This is a far, far better thing I do now than I have ever done. Rembrandt.'

Questions at an election meeting introduce the only 'joke' in the script.

'Does the continual watching of television affect the eyes?'

'Only if it's switched on. Next.'

He is asked: 'What do you intend to do about England entering into the European Common Market, thus bringing about a more sound economic structure of Europe without endangering our interest in Commonwealth trade and Imperial Preference?'

'Come now, sir,' he replies with dignity, 'this is no time for frivolous questions.'

Polling day finds him with a House of Commons badge already on his bike. He declines Sid's offer to beat up the other candidates. 'I careth not for what they say but I will defend with my life their right to say it. Beethoven.'

The results come through. Hancock has polled one.

He demands a recount.

Not even his friends voted for him.

'Oh well, if at first you don't succeed try, try, again. Rimsky Korsakov.'

As consolation, the local independent party send him 50 packets of cornflakes. He thinks he will have some. He takes a spoonful. He chokes. He has swallowed something. The doctor says that the X-ray shows that it appears to be a little plastic guardsman. And what's more, the doctor's afraid it is wedged and they cannot get it out.

Hancock must know how bad it is. 'You can tell me,' he says heroically, 'I can take it. I don't want you to lie to me. I want you to give it to me straight. What instrument is he playing?'

The answer is of course a trumpet.

'Stone me,' says Hancock, 'isn't it marvellous?'

Excerpt from 'Hancock' by Freddie Hancock & David Watham published by William Kimber & Co. Ltd.

de Emerald Oil

*or THE BEST OF THE IRISH JOKES**

Two Irishman were watching a John Wayne film on television. In one scene John Wayne was riding madly towards a cliff.
'I bet you £10 that he falls over the cliff', said one Irishman to the other.
'Done', said the second.
John Wayne rode straight over the cliff.
As the second Irishman handed over his £10, the first said, 'I feel a bit guilty about this. I've seen the film before'.
'So have I', said the second Irishman, 'but I didn't think he'd be fool enough to make the same mistake twice'.

□●□

A fellow was explaining to a Irishman how Nature sometimes compensates for a person's deficiences.
'For example', he told him, 'if a man is deaf, he may have keener sight, and if a man is blind, he may have a very keen sense of smell'.
'I think I see what you mean', said the Irishman, 'I've often noticed that if a man has one short leg, then the other one is always a little bit longer'.

□●□

Have you heard about the Irishman who cheated the railway?
He bought a return ticket to Dublin and didn't go back.

□●□

How do you recognise a Irish pirate?
He's got a patch over each eye.

□●□

A Irishman who had fallen into a lot of money, went to the doctor with an injured leg.
'That looks nasty' said the doctor, 'I'd better give you a local anaesthetic'.
'Hang the expense', said the Irishman, 'I'll have the imported one'.

□●□

Have you heard about the Irishwoman who tried to iron her curtains?
She fell out the window.

□●□

A Irishman's house caught fire, so he rushed to the near telephone kiosk and dialled very quickly.
'Hello, is that 999?'
'No. This is 998'.
'Well, would you nip in next door and tell them my house is on fire?'.

□●□

Have you heard about the expedition of Irishman who set out to climb Mount Everest?
They ran out of scaffolding thirty feet from the top.

'I'll never be able to understand', said a Ke man reading a newspaper, 'how people always seem to die in alphabetical order'.

□●□

Irishman viewing a broken window:-
'It's worse than I thought. It's broken on both sides'.

□●□

Did you hear about the Irishman who saw a notice reading:-
'Man Wanted For Robbery and Murder?'
He went in and applied for the job.

□●□

How can a 4 ft. 11½ ins. Irishman join the Guards?
Only if he lies about his height.

□●□

An American tourist was boasting to a Irishman about the fact that the Americans had just put a man on the moon.
'That's nothing,' said the Irishman, 'we have plans to land a man on the sun'.
'That's crazy', said the American, 'he would burn to a cinder before he got within a million miles of the sun'.
'We've thought of that too', said the Irishman, 'we're sending him at night'.

□●□

How do you keep a Irishman happy for an afternoon?
Write P.T.O. on both sides of a piece of paper.

□●□

One Irishman bet another that he couldn't carry him across Niagara Falls on a tightrope. After a hair-raising trip he made it to the other side. As one Irishman handed over the bet of £100 to the other he sighed 'I was sure I had won the bet when you wobbled halfway over'.

□●□

Then there was the Irishman who joined the 75th regiment of the army, to be near his brother who was in the 76th regiment.

□●□

Have you heard about the Irishman who went to a drive-in movie?
He didn't like the show so he slashed the seats.

A Irishman visited Harley Street and got an appointment with a famous plastic surgeon.
'Are you the famous plastic surgeon?' asked the Irishman.
'I am that', replied the plastic surgeon.
'In that case', said the Irishman, 'how much would it cost to have this plastic bucket mended?'

**passed by the Race Relations Board.*

TWO BY TWO

It's terrible what we do to animals — we eat them, chase them, ride them train them, **clothe** *them — remember the American story about the Society for the Prevention of Nude Horses? Not so way out when you think of all those poodles in their cute little knitted waistcoats and horses in blankets and even — may we be forgiven — elephants in drag. Cats — being cats — won't wear it, as anyone will know who's tried to put as much as a bandage on a feline tail. Last time I tried, the confounded cat streaked straight up to the top of the nearest tree, bandage unrolling as it went like a miniature loo roll in the breeze.*

And when we aren't trying to put something on them or over on them, we demand instant affection and absolute obedience from our animals — though whether we get it or not is another matter. I must say it's hard sometimes to believe that that **is** *the light of love in my tortoise's eye — I often feel it only raises that iron shutter of an eyelid to see where it's going, and the rate it moves it doesn't need to do even that very often. As for its sex — who knows. I go along with Ogden Nash on this one:*

The turtle lives amid plated decks
Which practically conceal its sex.
Isn't it clever of the turtle
In such a fix to be so fertle?

K.B.

One-Pupmanship

by EPHRAIM KISHON

One evening not long ago my wife decided that the children wanted a dog. I categorically refused.

"Again?" I asked. "We discussed this before, didn't we?"

"Only on a trial basis," replied the woman, "for the children."

"Naturally. But afterward we'll get attached to it and won't be able to get rid of it."

The children broke into wild sobs, viz: Daddydogdaddydogdaddydog. A certain compromise appeared on the horizon.

"O.K.," I said, "I'll buy a dog, Which kind?"

"Pure-bred," my wife said. "With a pedigree. What we need is an obedient dog with a sharp bark, but quiet, non-chewing, house-broken, and under no circumstances a bitch, because they are in heat twice a year. I also don't want a male dog because they chase the bitches, but a pure-bred dog whose ancestors were registered for several generations with a reputable veterinarian, because only these are worth the price one pays for them."

"All right," I said. "So this is the dog the children want?"

"Yes. Go and look around. But for God's sake don't buy the first dog they offer you."

So I went to town looking for action. On the way, a man with a severe cough asked me if I was looking for a dog. He said he had one just around the corner, in his garden. I went with him, and we found among the bushes in a used shoebox a pup with curly hair, bow legs and a black nose with a lot of pink spots. The dog was chewing on its own tail, and as soon as he spotted us he jumped up at me and licked my shoes with gusto. I became attached to him right away.

"What's his name?" I asked.

"Who knows?" Coughs answered. "You can have it."

"is he pure-bred?"

"What do you mean pure-bred?" the man flared up."This dog is made up of quite a few breeds, so for me he is very pure-bred. The main thing is he barks. Do you want him or don't you?"

I saw that he was angry, so I agreed. Also, as I said, I had become attached to the dog.

"How much do you want for him?"

"Nothing. Only take it away."

He wrapped up the pup in a newspaper, pushed it in my hands and shoved us out of the garden. But I had hardly gone two steps when I suddenly remembered my wife and drew up short. This—it flashed through my mind—this is not exactly the dog we had discussed only a few minutes ago. What's more, should I bring it back home, both of us would be kicked down the stairs. I looked inside the newspaper. He trembled slightly and only his head protruded from yesterday's news. Then I realized that as a matter of fact he had a pink nose with black spots. No, this wouldn't pass muster at home.

I hurried back to the coughing man.

"I'm not going home now," I lied. "I'll fetch him later on in the afternoon."

"Listen," the man puffed, "I'm ready to pay you a few pounds . . ."

"That won't be necessary. I've already become attached to him. I'll fetch him soon, don't worry."

"Well," the woman asked, "any luck?"

This was a very primitive trap, I must say.

"You don't buy a dog as quick as that," I said coolly. "I consulted several experts today and they offered me a few Scotch terriers and a rattler, but they were not pure-bred enough for me."

I was not quite sure whether a breed called "rattler" really existed, but somehow it sounded credible.

Anyway, the wife saw that I was taking the dog-buying business very seriously.

"No need to hurry," she remarked. "After all, how many times in a lifetime does one buy a dog?"

"of course," I agreed. "I've seen a few ads in the newspaper. Tomorrow I'll go and make a few cautious inquiries."

Next day I went straight to the beach and frolicked about in the waves. I even played a few games of beach tennis with the lifeguard. At lunchtime, on the way home, I made a quick visit to my dog at the coughing man's and had fun with him for a few minutes in the garden. He was very happy to see me, the dog, and licked me all over, and then I noticed that even the topography of his tongue was very indistinct. This dog has not a single pigment of nobility in him, I sadly decided. How will I bring him home?

"Tomorrow," I said to Coughs, "tomorrow it's a sure thing. We are getting anti-rabies shots today, the whole family, and day after tomorrow we'll be safe."

"The ads in the paper are not worth the ink they are printed with," I related to the wife. "They are offering me all sorts of mongrels. That's not for me."

"Still," the woman asked, her inquisitive eyes sweeping my tense features, "what have you actually seen?"

She forgot that I am a poet of sorts.

"I have seen a Yorkshire poodle, not bad at all, in Ramat Gan," I told her dreamily, "but his pedigree reached back only four generations. Besides, I couldn't rid myself of the impression that several of his sisters and brothers were inbred."

"So what?" the wife retorted. "That's quite natural with dogs."

I raised my voice. "Not with me! With me the word 'pedigree' still has a precise meaning, if you don't mind. Either I find us an aristocrat, or else the hell with it."

The wife looked at me with new admiration in her eyes, the like of which I have never seen before.

"Maybe you are right," the little one whispered. "To tell the truth you surprise me pleasantly. I thought you'd bring home the first dog that crossed your path."

"You see?" I berated her, almost choking with fury, "we have been married for twelve years and you still don't know me! If you must know, I am driving to Haifa tomorrow morning to consult Dr. Manczel, the number-one expert on German shepherd dogs."

Next morning I took leave of my family and went straight to Max. So help me, he's a really nice dog. He literally jumped at my collar out of sheer exuberance when I entered the coughing man's garden on tiptoe. I intended to teach the dog some elementary rules of behaviour, such as jumping over hurdles, catching criminals and such things. But Max was quite unteachable, to the extent that for a few minutes I even regretted that I had become attached to him. To top it all, Coughs suddenly showed up and kicked up a row that he would toss the bloody bitch out of the garden if I didn't take her immediately and added a few sentences in Polish.

"Excuse me," I said to him, "did you say 'bitch' just now?"

"What's the difference? Take it away!"

Max looked at me with her sad eyes and her tail wagged her muscular body.

"Why?" her glance said. "Why aren't we going?"

"I'm working on it," I signaled to her reassuringly. "I'm working on it."

At home I dropped onto my couch completely exhausted from the strain of the long drive.

"I talked to Dr. Manczel," I summed up the situation." She showed me a number of fairly pure-bred dogs, but my instinct warned me not to fall into her trap."

"Aren't you exaggerating a bit?" the little one asked. "No one is perfect."

"I won't tolerate compromises," I shouted. "I decided, woman, to buy a thoroughly pure-bred dog from a famous Swiss kennel."

"How much is this going to cost?"

"Don't ask me! But since we are doing it, let's go the whole hog. I won't settle for any less. I chose a dark-white miniature schnauzer. On his father's side he goes back right to Frederick the Great; on his mother's side he is related to Excellenz von Stukler. He's as aristocratic as can be. He's even a hemophiliac."

"Excellent," the wife gushed, though I detected a certain tiredness in her voice. "But aren't they going to cheat us?"

"Cheat me? Don't you see how carefully I check everything? From the airport the dog goes straight to the laboratory; then all his documents will undergo a close scrutiny. No one is going to pull a fast one on me."

"I think you are a maniac," the wife opinioned. "Why can't you make up your mind? After all, it's only a dog."

The next three days were very difficult ones. Coughs listened to my excuses behind narrowing eyes. He wouldn't hear of my delaying the dog's homecoming again, though I claimed that I was coordinating it with the upcoming birthday of my little daughter. He asked to see her identity card. Then he grabbed Max and threw her after me over the fence, while shouting obscene remarks about crooks born in the Balkans. I shushed the frightened bitch with a few tender strokes, then hurried to the fence, threw her back into the garden and fled for my life.

"Max has been delayed because of the custom men's strike," I informed the wife. "His history is at present being checked in the genealogical institute in Jerusalem."

"You," the woman fumed, "you and your morbid pedantry!"

But I could see that her resistance had greatly weakened. Max was waiting for me at the street corner, lonely and pathetic. That villain had chased her out of the garden between paroxysms of coughing. I bought the poor little dog a new leather collar with a lot of brass knobs and took her home.

"Straight from Switzerland," I introduced her. "Max."

The whole family looked at her respectfully. This was the first time they had come across a foreign-bred miniature schnauzer who was a real Cohen from the genealogical point of view.

"Beautiful," the wife mumbled. "Really, it has been worth while waiting for him."

She was already deeply attached to him. And indeed, he is a wonderful bitch, Max is. Her tail is in perpetual movement, like a metronome, and her little eyes shine with wisdom till you have the feeling that she will start speaking any moment. Though personally I hope she won't open her mouth.

Excerpt from 'Wise Guy Solomon' published by Atheneum, New York

Perishers

Drawn by Dennis Collins
Written by Morris Dodd

Dishing the Dirt

TO TELL THE truth I'm still not quite sure how we came to acquire this horse, though as I sit here reconstructing the crime, omitting no detail however small, I'm drawn increasingly to the conclusion that I was, once again, the victim of a cunning plot concocted by the monstrous regiment with whom I live.

I do recall that prior to the offence there'd been much talk of horses but then in my house there's always much talk of horses, largely because my elder daughter is a child who sees life exclusively in equine terms.

To you or me a western film, for instance, resolves itself into a conflict between, say, John Wayne and assorted heavies but to her it's far more complicated and she may spend the entire movie trying to decide whether the dapple grey stallion is, or is not, fractionally more sympathetic than the roan mare. And when eventually Wayne blasts his adversaries out of their saddles she's likely to round on him indignantly, saying: "What did he do that for? Who's going to look after their horses now they're dead?"

In her view the human race is divided into those who are likely to be nice to horses and those who are not, which makes me and my ambivalent attitude somewhat suspect. But at least you know where you are with my elder daughter and when she sleep-walked into the parental bedroom like a diminutive Lady Macbeth, saying in sepulchral tones, "You didn't clear the jump, did you?", I knew at once that in her dreams the whole family had been taking part in the Grand National and I, as usual, had failed to make it over Becher's Brook.

However. I got home one evening and there on the doorstep was the regiment — one wife, two daughters — puce with excitement and yelling, "We've got a horse;" like a chorus of racecourse tipsters.

"It's a palomina called Loner and she dishes," said my elder daughter who, it transpired, was the nominal owner of this beast though I, of course, was to have the privilege of paying for it.

"And she's got cow hocks," said my younger daughter.

"And an egg-butt snaffle," said my wife, at which point I naturally drew the line. "Egbert who?" I said. "No, sod it, I'm not taking on a bloody stable lad as well. Besides, nobody's called Egbert Snaffle. It's obviously a pseudonym. He's probably wanted by the police. No, no, a rotten horse is one thing but I'm not employing a fugitive from justice."

Whereupon, with the intellectual derision of one who had herself been apprised of the facts only five minutes earlier, my wife explained that this snaffle was something you stuck in the horse's mouth and then she glossed so lightly over the dishing and the cow hocks that I realised the animal was practically an invalid and possibly even bed-ridden and finally she played her trump card. "Well I couldn't resist her," she said, defiantly. "She's got such lovely long eyelashes, like a pantomime horse."

"Do you mean" I said, "that you bought this equine cripple because it fluttered its eyelashes at you? How much was it?"

"Oh, very reasonable," she said and revealed the price.

"That's reasonable?" I said.

"Think of the manure," she said and in fact I was thinking of the manure. At this time of year I'm obliged to think of little else because my wife's idea of a well-tended vegetable garden is one that's knee-deep in horse-shit through which the occasional plant fights its way into daylight, choking for breath and holding its nose.

This hadn't affected me much over the last year or so because she'd been working an abandoned manure mine which she found in the corner of a field but now she's almost exhausted the seam and lately she's been scattering hints to the effect that anyone who really cared for her — a devoted husband perhaps — would happily scour the highways and byways with a plastic bag and a shovel collecting horse-droppings for her.

Thus the suggestion that I should regard this horse not simply as a horse but as a fully-equipped, mobile manure factory turned the trick and soon afterwards it took up residence in a local field, since when it has dominated the spare time and conversation of both my daughters but has produced very little manure.

My wife says you can't rush these things and it's unreasonable to expect too rapid a return on investment. But sometimes, as I reflect on the initial price of the horse and the cost of keeping it in idleness and luxury, it seems to me that for a much smaller outlay I could have manure delivered daily to the door by a liveried chauffeur in a Rolls-Royce.

BARRY NORMAN

"Charles! Did you ask anyone to meet you here this morning?"

from 'Thelwell Country' published by Methuen Ltd.

keeping one jump ahead

Tonight we tell the story of Lester Fester, who, from humble beginnings and no education, fought his way up through the jungle of our society to become an internationally respected politician and statesman.

Not such an unusual story, you may say, but Lester Fester was a horse.

I am Lester Fester, now Baron Fester of Piggot . . . friends call me Lester Piggott, which confuses the hell out of everybody . . . anybody got an apple? Oh, it doesn't matter. My biographer, Ferdinand Chuff takes up the story . . . not a master of English, but not bad for a trained seal.

Lester Fester was born at an early . . . born at . . . hang on, it's impossible to talk with a ball balanced on your nose. That's better . . . anybody got a raw fish? Oh, it doesn't matter. Lester Fester was born in Barnet, the result of a union between an underguarded Arab stallion and an oversexed milkman's mare. His father left his mother shortly afterwards to run fourth in the St. Leger. His mother's owner was done for fiddling with his yoghourts, she was transferred to Harpenden and Lester was left to fend for himself.

I was a wild child . . . many's the time I was reprimanded for kicking over the traces . . . and the chairs and the table and the stable lad.

Headmaster, I can't cope with Fester anymore . . . when he's not biting the monitor, he's racing down the corridor . . . not only that, he's got Gordon Richards up.

That's as may be, Miss Firkinshaw but I've got his exam results here . . . that damn horse has got nine Hay Levels.

When I left school, I applied for a job at a stud farm but I failed the entrance exam due to nerves . . . you know how it is. However, a friendly ferret I met on a railway train, persuaded me to try the law.

My name is Rudyard Affidavit Q.C. Not impressed? Well, I'm a tortoise, so there! I met Lester one day when he was grazing in Lincoln's Inn Fields. After he'd trodden on me, we struck up a friendship . . . I well remember his first case . . .

(ECHO) And I say to you, ladies and gentlemen and hamsters of the jury, that the prosecution have completely failed to prove that my client, Neville Chamberlain, is guilty of smuggling bits of paper into the country. And I recommend that you let him leave this court without a stain on his umbrella!

There is the sound of a seal clapping.

Usher, remove that seal!

Not going to be easy your honour, I'm a Cabbage White Butterfly.

Oh well . . . pollenate off.

Lester went on to triumph after triumph . . . you may recall the case of Hargreaves versus Rex . . . Rex was so annoyed at losing, he bit the foreman of the jury in the leg. At the height of his meteoric career, Lester received a summons to Ten Downing Street . . .

Well, Fester, we're very impressed with your record . . . we'd like you to stand for Parliament . . . oh and while you're here, have you got anything for my rhubarb?

Lester took his seat in the house but continued his legal career, starring in many horse trials . . . he was responsible on one memorable occasion for getting Princess Ann fined thirty bob. The people of his home town of Barnet were so proud of him that they wanted to make him Mayor but he refused to have the operation.

In 1960, romance entered my life . . . during Badminton week, my eye was taken by a young filly who had just thrown Harvey Smith three times. I admired her spirit and her good taste and we fell into conversation and a ditch.

Lester and Dymphna were married at the romantically named Chapel of the Oats by a close friend of the Archbishop of Canterbury's . . . a wallaby. At the close of the service, he jumped over the happy couple and punched the organist in the mouth.

My life followed a logical pattern, many honours were bestowed upon me, including a Gannex horse blanket and a life peerage.

"A horse in the House of Lords?" you may be saying, dear listener, "Why have we not heard of this before?" Nobody's noticed, really . . . the place has been full of asses for years.

MARMADUKE

by Brad Anderson & Dorothy Leeming

"Other dogs bring their leashes for a walk. . . . HE brings the car keys for a ride!"

"We're having a circus and we need a tiger!"

"Good boy! Now keep him there till I go get some money!"

"Why shouldn't he feel secure? He outweighs me by 40 pounds!"

Published by Wyndham Publications Ltd.

Feathered Friends

Birds have helped man in many ways. For example, pigeons enabled man to send messages by air long before birds inspired him to invent the airplane, and they continued in service even afterward. Carrier pigeons were used as late as World War I. But air mail—or the pigeon post, as it was called—really started with the Egyptians, who first noticed the unusual homing instinct of the pigeon and decided to put it to work for their own purposes.

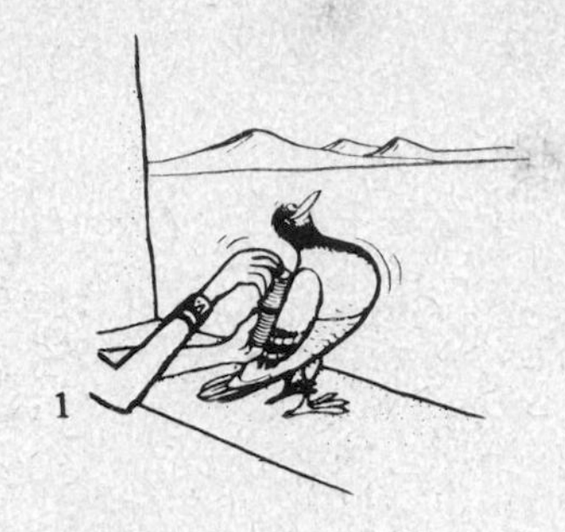

1

2

3

The pigeon flew through searing heat . . .

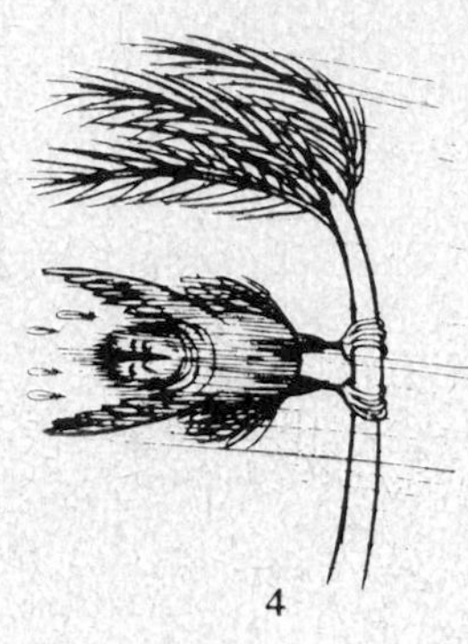

4

. . . bucked mighty winds . . .

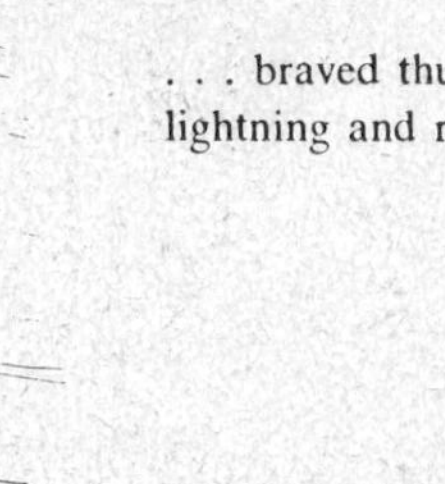

. . . braved thunder, lightning and rain . . .

5

. . . withstood hail . . .

6

7

. . . avoided birds of prey . . .

8

. . . dodged hunters . . .

. . . and made soft landings . . .

9

. . . before completing his appointed round . . .

10

. . . and bringing the message to its proper destination, thus affecting the destiny of men and nations.

11

Excerpt from 'Gurney's Guide to Feathered Friends' by Erico & Nancy Gurney, published by Frederick Muller Ltd.

WINE & DINE

HOST: "Dammit man, you've just belched in front of my wife".
GUEST: "I do apologise, my dear fellow. I didn't realise it was her turn".

Drinking is drinking wherever you are, and the results are always the same—too much saki is just as bad as more than enough ouso or retsina (and they even **sound** *nauseating). But eating abroad is another matter; you either come back convinced that there's no cooking like English cooking (though you can read that the wrong way), or else you can't wait to pin everyone's ears back with stories of the fantastic food you ate in Outer Mongolia or wherever we can now be packaged. Worse, you try re-creating the sort of meals you had there, and you always end up with something even the cat won't eat. For one thing, you're not going to find the right ingredients — after all, your friendly neighbourhood butcher doesn't often come up with a nice cut of octopus (though mine has a nasty line in* **Save Our Dumb Friends' League** *collecting boxes and* **Saved by the Blood of the Lamb** *texts among his carcases). And even if you could get the right sort of weird and wonderful meat, what do you do for a herb that only grows wild in the swamps of Bulgaria, or for the way-out veg. that has a two-day season once every five years and only then in a remote part of Abyssinia?*

Better go back to the old fish and chips, and keep your memories beautiful. *K.B.*

Confessions of a Pudding Man...

...alias ROBERT MORLEY

I am a pudding man. Nothing depresses me more than a meal which doesn't finish with one. 'Just coffee for me, thanks,' is not a phrase in my book. However boring the occasion, I perk up when they wheel in the sweet trolley. I inspect it as I would a guard of honour, I insist the jellies should be standing to attention, the rhubarb, although I never touch it, pale pink, the chocolate sauce dark and mysterious. I cannot contemplate a spoilt trifle. 'What was in that?' I ask, as I wave away the half-filled dish and wait for the replacement. Sometimes there are several trolleys going the rounds. It is as well to inspect them all. They are seldom identical. The first lesson I taught my children was never to show your hand when being served from a trolley. Never ask for a little of that and a little of that, please. If you have decided on profiteroles and syllabub, encourage the waiter to pile your plate with the former, and only when he has put back the spoon, suddenly, and on the spur of the fork, as it were, demand the syllabub.

Because I am a great artist myself, I know the disappointment of rejection. I know what it is like to 'bang on the slap' and find the house empty. I know what it must be like for a chef to send out a Creme Honorê and have it returned untouched. When no one bought his paintings, Gauguin, or was it Van Gogh, cut off his own ear. A kitchen is full of knives. I must put no similar temptation in the way of a pastrycook.

I look forward to the petit fours, often nibbling the spun sugar in the swan's beak, or breaking off a piece of the basket and chewing the wicker work. I am not fond of marzipan. It is not a medium in which a chef does his finest work. The best sweet trolleys are always to be found in Italian restaurants, the most meagre in Indian ones. The two finest puddings I have ever tasted are the circular mille feuilles obtainable at the Chateau de Madrid and an Orange Boodle Fool my daughter occasionally makes at the weekends when we have company.

I am a lifelong enemy of tapioca, but every now and then am seduced by a prune. I am still fond of a good meringue, but never hope to taste again quite the perfection of my grandmother's. I was smaller in those days, but a meringue should always be judged, like a vegetable marrow, by its size.

Of my schooldays I remember with pleasure only the tuck shop on the days I could afford a tenpenny mess (one banana, two scoops ice-cream and extra cream). I don't say I was happy then, but I was a little less miserable. While others dreamt of success on the playing fields, my private fantasy was a box of milk flake bars to myself.

For a time after I left school I was hooked on Walnut Whips, but ever afterwards have been a milk chocolate addict. I share my craving with one of my cats. Together we prowl the house, searching for the cache where my wife has hidden the bars she buys for the children. When we discover the hoard, we demolish it. Naturally, my share is larger than Tom's, but once we have awoken our taste buds, nothing can stop us. I have even known Tom to eat the silver paper. I have left many things unfinished in my life, but never a bar of chocolate. I haven't a wisdom-tooth in my head, but thank the Lord I still have a sweet one.

This excerpt from 'A Musing Morley' by Robert Morley (Robson Books Ltd.) was first published in Punch Magazine.

CALMAN

From The Art of Coarse Drinking

By Michael Green

Anyone drinking with Americans must remember they are totally incapable of drinking in moderation. The quiet half-pint is as unknown in America as the small automobile. Assume, therefore, if invited to any function involving drink by an American that the place will be swimming in the hard stuff. Beer is not really considered alcoholic, which is hardly surprising since it's so highly-chilled as to have all alcohol and flavour driven out.

Americans are also afraid of drinks in their pure form. Be prepared for continual attempts to adulterate liquor by adding something or turning it into a cocktail. Even Scotch will have ice in it.

Small measures are unknown. As the Americans are very generous hosts one's glass is permanently full and hosts are constantly urging guests to drink a little so they can put some more in. To avoid giving offence, I keep hiding my glass at American parties, with the result there is a trail of half-empty Scotch glasses round the room. They must find them afterwards in every nook and cranny—stuffed down the grand piano, behind the radiators, on the window sills, even inside vases. Even then I'm awash in 30 minutes.

This habit once got me into trouble. I used to be invited regularly to the house of some American friends employed at the London Embassy, and one day the wife rang me up in great distress.

"Mike," she said, "you know all about indoor plants and things don't you?"

Well, I didn't, but on the strength of having kept a rubber plant alive for a year I had some reputation so I said yes, and she continued, "Well I wish you'd come over and look at my plants. They've all suddenly died."

I must say she hadn't exaggerated. Entering her house was like looking at a Goya painting of a massacre. All these little plants were sprawled all over their pots in contorted positions as if they had died in agony, and some of them had gone black.

I then realised what had happened. For six months I'd been pouring those vast American Scotches she served into the flower-pots and those poor little plants had been poisoned by whisky. Fortunately I had the wit to say, "It looks like Fuller's disease to me. You'll have to change the soil and start again."

This left me with the problem of where to dispose of my unwanted drinks in future (she immediately thanked me by giving me a Scotch big enough for six). For several parties after that I was reduced to all sorts of devices like slinking out of the room with my glass and tipping the surplus out of the window. Even that led to trouble because a neighbour told my host. "That must have been some party you had yesterday. Scotch was pouring out of the windows and dripping down the walls . . ."

Extract published by Curtis-Brown Ltd.

1964 by E. C. Publications Inc. from Mad Magazines

In 1955, when Ben Renfro realised that the sheriff's men were closing in on his house, where he was making illicit liquor, in Chattanooga, Tennessee, he quickly poured the stuff down the kitchen sink to destroy the evidence. The sheriff got his proof just the same. Anticipating what Renfro might do, he was waiting with a jug to catch the liquor at the other end of the waste pipe.

"WHICH want me to do a test on furniture polishes!"

"Bloody Mary, please – group 'O'."

A friend of Bill Hawkins knocked on his door one day. 'Where's Bill?' he asked his wife.

'He's just died,' replied the woman. 'He went down the garden to cut a cabbage for lunch, tripped over the wheelbarrow, knocked his head on the shed door, fell over the motor-mower, and the garden fork went clean through his heart.'

'Good heavens! What did you do?'

'Only thing I *could* do. Opened a tin of peas.'

*

Definition of a fat man: Food gone to waist.

*

"I think Case No. 14 is regaining consciousness," reported a nurse in an alcoholics' ward. "He's just tried to blow the froth off his medicine."

*

"Hello, old man, you look happy."

"Yes, I've just got a bottle of whiskey for the wife."

"Well, that sounds a fair swap."

"Will that be all, sir?"

Many of the best and wittiest stories are told (and re-told) by some big or biggish wig after some big dinner or other when, amid the rumble of good conversation and overloaded stomachs, everyone sits back, lights a dirty great cigar and waits to be amused. Nothing, it seems, helps the food and drink down better than a good laugh. So next time you've downed the last of the pud., why not try one of these . . .

After Dinner Mints I.

A gourmet attended a banquet in London and heard from other gastronomical colleagues of a fabulous dish called Poy. Apparently you could only obtain it from one place in the world. Full of curiosity, he inquired where it was. None of his colleagues had had it but all had heard of it. One knew where the village was where it could be obtained. "You go up to Katmandu, up and over the pass, turn right in the middle of the highest village and you will find it at the second monastery on the left." The gourmet organised an expedition. He flew to Katmandu, hired guides and carriers and set off. After months of climbing up mountains and down valleys and up mountains again he came to the monastery. He rang the great bell and a monk answered. "I have come all the way from London to sample your world-famed dish known as Poy," he said. "That is curious", replied the monk. "The cook himself comes from London. I did not know his dish, which he calls Poy, had become world famous. Which of the two will you sample, Shepherd's Poy or Steak and Kidney Poy?"

There was a member of the House of Lords who suspected that a trainer had been doping. So for months whenever the trainer had a runner, his Lordship was there, watching every movement. There came a day when the trainer had a filly which was not much fancied and, after he saddled her, his Lordship noticed the trainer take a little box from his pocket, take something out, and gave it to the filly to swallow. His Lordship pounced — "What's that?" "Oh my Lord" said the trainer, "it's just a little sweetmeat — nothing at all. I'll have one and you have one."

The trainer swallowed the tablet and his Lordship found himself doing the same. A few moments later the jockey came into the ring and the trainer said "Take her down very quietly, jump her off, lie on the rails—about fourth—and when you come to the straight pull her out and go on and win. If anything passes you it will either be his Lordship or me."

The after-dinner speaker had been introduced in flattering terms. On rising to reply, he said: "Such an introduction makes me pray two prayers for forgiveness: the first for my introducer, because he has told so many lies; the second for myself, because I have enjoyed it so much."

There is a story carried down in all Bar Messes where lawyers meet of the deaf judge, deaf defendant and deaf plaintiff. The judge took his seat, looked at the plaintiff and said: "You begin". The plaintiff said: "My Lord, my claim is for rent". The judge, not having heard a single word, looked at the defendant, and said: "What do you say?" The defendant, also not having heard, said: "My Lord, how can that be so when I grind my corn at night?" The judge retorted: "This is a very difficult problem. I have formed an opinion and I am immensely impressed by the claims. I think she is the mother of both of you and you should both maintain her".

An Ambassador once travelled from Paris to Istanbul on the Orient Express, and was bitten by bugs on the way. He sent a strong complaint to the Company, and in reply received a letter stating that they were horrified that so eminent a person should have suffered in this way; that such a thing had never, in their experience, happened before; that they were taking stringent measures to prevent any possibility of a recurrence; and that they begged him to accept their humblest apologies.

All very proper. But unhappily the clerk who dealt with the complaint, by inadvertence, attached to this reply the Ambassador's original letter of complaint, across which someone had scribbled "Usual bug letter please."

A certain Vicar used to boast that he belonged to no political party and no one knew for which party he voted at a General Election. The only possible clue available to anyone was his insistence on choosing the first hymn at a Sunday Service after a by-election.

If a Conservative won he would choose the hymn: "Now thank we all our God."

If a Labour Candidate won he would choose the hymn: "Oh! God our help in ages past."

If a Liberal won he would choose the hymn: "God moves in a mysterious way, His wonders to perform."

A FEW WORDS FROM

MANNING and CROMPTON

From Wheeltappers & Shunters Social Club Members' Handbook published by Pentagon books.

The Daily Blooper

DURING the past few days three bicycles have been stolen from Exeter streets. The police consider that a bicycle thief is at work.

Western Morning News

U.S. Air Force General Don Flickinger said last night that all chimpanzees used in space flights would be volunteers. He was asked how chimpanzees could volunteer. He replied: 'We hold an apple in one hand and a banana in the other. If they choose the banana, they are judged to have volunteered. They almost always choose the banana.'

Daily Express

Customers who consider our waitresses uncivil should see the manager

Notice in cafe

Dear Sirs,
In buying your biscuits I have noticed that the top biscuit in the packet is nearly always broken. I am therefore writing to suggest that in future you should leave out the top biscuit in each packet.
Yours truly, Mrs N. Jackson

Letter to biscuit manufacturer.

Farmers in bad odour with townspeople

Liverpool Daily Post

Once you have dealt with us you will recommend others.

Advert in *East Kent Mercury*

Nudist welfare man's model wife fell for the Chinese hypnotist from the Co-op bacon factory

NEWS OF THE WORLD

STRIP CLUBS SHOCK

Magistrates may act on indecent shows.

Daily Mirror

It was just after the assembled guests had toasted the bride that her wedding gown caught fire. She was not seriously hurt, and the reception continued.

Visiting hours in women's colleges should be made equal to those in men's colleges. There is little conceivable reason for prohibiting men visitors in women's rooms.

YOU too can know the confidence and comfort of a firm denture if you sprinkle your plate every morning with Dr Thompson's Powder. You can laugh, talk and enjoy your meals all day long. Forget your false teeth, start using Dr Thompson's Today.

Advert. in Daily paper

Something New Which No Motorist Should Be Without. We offer you THE SELF-GRIP WENCH.

Advert. in motoring paper

WHY BREAK YOUR CHINA WASHING UP?
Do it automatically in a dishwasher!
From John R. Fordham, Epping. 'Phone 33.
Established 1923.

Advert in *Surrey Mirror*

To serve, dip moulds in water to loosen the contents and serve with passion fruit and cream. British housewives can substitute pineapple, cherries or apricots for passion.

Romford Recorder

The concert held in the Good Templars' Hall was a great success . . . Special thanks are due to the Vicar's daughter who laboured the whole evening at the piano, which as usual fell upon her.

South African paper

The community is rapidly becoming more self-supporting—18,000 dozen corsets were locally made during the last twelve months.

Scottish paper

The service was conducted by the Rev Charles Harris MA, the bridegroom. The wedding was of a quiet nature owing to the recent death of the bride.

Blackpool Times

Snap!

All Photographs from Rex Features

BEHIND THE SCENES

Almost everyone who is anyone in the showbiz world has had a lot of hairy experiences on their way up — which they manage quite often to turn into something funny. This is not easy when you're hard-up and hungry and playing to audiences who seem as dumb as you're afraid **you** *are. Most of their stories ring true — like the story of Bessie Bellwood, one of the fruitiest of the old Music Hall performers who was playing a riotous East End date. The audience was so rowdy and raucous that it was impossible to hear even Bessie's powerful tones above it — until a tremendous voice from the gallery suddenly roared out "Why don't you all shut up and give the old cow a chance?" The audience quietened down considerably, and "Thank you, sir" Bessie called up to the gallery "it's nice to know there's at least one gentleman in the house."*

And she's not the only performer to whom "a funny thing happened"!! *K.B.*

A FUNNY THING HAPPENED

To Eric & Ernie..

There was old Tattersall who did a speciality vent act with life-size dummies that he built himself. Worked by clockwork, they breathed, they walked about. I wouldn't be surprised if they even had a bit on the side, though they were usually Chelsea pensioners and their ninety-year-old molls.

There was a wonderful story about the time Tattersall was playing the Theatre Royal, Hanley. On the Saturday night after the last show, he came out of the theatre, packed his dummies into his station wagon and was about to leave when he saw Lynda and Lana, two dancers, standing forlornly in the rain waiting for a taxi.

'Would you like a lift?' he enquired gallantly.

'Oh, thank you,' the girls said.

'You're a bit crowded,' said Lynda.

'Not at all, my dear. All we need do is stow my gear a little more sensibly.'

With that he took his dummy old lady out of the station wagon, propped her up against the wall near the stage-door, loaded the girls' props and luggage into the vehicle, got in with the girls, and drove off to Newcastle, leaving the old lady by the stage-door.

Meanwhile she had been found by the Leeds police. They spoke to her but she refused to answer. The Leeds Royal Infirmary medical staff were consulted, an ambulance team arrived, they tried to wake her.

'She's breathing, so she must be alive,' said the doctor.

He shook her. She did not respond.

'We can of course arrest her,' said a young constable.

'On what charge?' his superior demanded.

'What about loitering with intent?'

'You bloody fool—and make ourselves the laughing stock of the Constabulary? Does the old dear look as though she could do *anything,* much less commit a felony?'

'Causing an obstruction?' suggested another constable.

'The owner of the property will have to make a complaint. And he won't because he would be made to look an ogre in the local papers.'

'Leave her alone,' said a passer-by. 'She's doing nobody any harm.'

'But it's raining. She must be cold and hungry. We can't leave her here. She looks like my mother, God bless her soul.'

So it went on until a telegram arrived from Newcastle, and the police, very red-faced, took over the dummy and lodged it in the left-luggage office at Leeds Central Station.

There was always something happening at Blackpool to make life interesting. As for practical jokes, one of the funniest I remember was when we got hold of a life-sized ventriloquist's dummy and put it in the pro's loo at the Central Pier—there was only one loo backstage for everybody. We pulled down the dummy's trousers and in the first hour or so several girls backed out with red faces. It wasn't long before we guessed there was one girl who was really bursting to go—after about her third attempt we heard her saying to the others that she suspected the 'person' in the toilet was really somebody's idea of a joke.

Promptly we whipped the dummy out and Eric went in and waited. The girl with the anxious bladder tried again. Eric let her open the door, then gave an 'Oops!' which sent her flying back to their dressing-room.

After a while Eric knocked on the door and called the girl's name.

'Yes?'

'The coast is clear, darling.'

I'll kill you!' she said.

Extract from 'Eric & Ernie' by Morecambe & Wise published by W. H. Allen & Co. Ltd.

A FUNNY THING HAPPENED

to Cardew Robinson..

I sometimes think about my early days as a humble member of the Charles Denville Repertory Company at the Attercliffe Palace Theatre, Sheffield, and of some of the many things which went wrong during that particular season of old time melodrama. Small wonder really when it's considered that we usually did two plays a week, so that our knowledge of each was consequently sketchy.

Our first production was a famous old tear-jerker. "The Story of the Rosary". As the Hero's Best Friend, I was fighting by his side, when, in the heat of the first night battle his false teeth suddenly fell out on to the stage. In a single magnificent movement, he bent down on one knee, while still engaging his adversary with his sword arm, and swept them back into his mouth with the other hand, stage dust and all!

I personally have had more than my share of misadventures, such as the time I had to unlock a stage bedroom door and found I had lost the key somewhere in the lining of my pocket; and the occasion when the theatre cat walked straight through the prop fire in the drawing room set and joined me in the middle of the stage forcing me to utter the dreadful line. "This is a monologue, not a catalogue!"; not to mention the first public dress rehearsal of 'Camelot' at Drury Lane when the massive old English sheep dog which accompanied my first entrance as King Pellinore was overcome with stage fright and disgraced itself right over the orchestra pit, nearly precipitating a musicians strike. And there were especially many of these little moments during our production of "Frankenstein", in which I played The Monster, would you believe. The management, for once, really lashed out on my ensemble. I had a perfect copy of the Karloff wig; the bolts through neck and wrists; and huge boots, which with the large high wig built up my height to about 6 feet ten inches. With my aquiline nose broadened by nose paste, and grease paint stitches all over my face I finished my make-up as a ghastly but pretty accurate reproduction of the great Boris in the original film. As I was admiring myself in my dressing room mirror, there was a knock on the door. Without thinking, I called "Come in", and there entered a teenage female cousin of mine named Ellen. She had been passing through Sheffield and had called at the Stage Door to see me without even being aware which play we were doing on that particular night. She had then been directed to my room, but not enlightened. As she came in I turned, rose, and walked towards her. She gave one shrill scream and fainted. I managed to revive her before facing my first night audience with renewed confidence. And on the whole I was very happy clomping about as a monster. In spite of little incidents such as the time when I dropped my head in my hands in shame at my hideous appearance and felt my false nose fall off. I caught it neatly and managed to stick it back on before raising my head again. Alas, as soon as I did my audience shrieked uncontrollably, but with laughter, not fright. I had put the nose back the wrong way up and it was pointing skywards.

I also had rather a trying time with the racing pigeon in the cage. It had been loaned to us by a stage hand to play the small but important part of a caged dove which is released by The Monster in an unexpected fit of benevolence, doves being rather thin on the ground in that part of Sheffield, or in the air too for that matter. I was directed to give it a good throw towards the wings and then pretend to watch it fly away to freedom.

"Gie it a reet good throw son", said its owner, "it's got a bit of trouble with its wing like, it won't go far."

First night nerves, plus natural tender feelings inhibited my throwing arm and the bird barely reached the wings. So that when I was watching the imaginary dove soaring away in the distance, the actual pigeon was starting to walk back on stage. I had to push it away with my big boot.

"I *told* you to gie it a good throw lad" the stage hand said sadly, after the first house was over." It's poorly; it won't fly away, don't you worry."

So at the 2nd house I really let go with that bird. My action must have had a quick curative effect. Suddenly it stopped acting the dove and reverted to being a racing pigeon. Not a poorly one either. It swooped out over the audience, then back on stage, and finally perched on top of a stage flat, visible to the audience, but just out of my reach. It continued to regard me sardonically while I gazed out into the wings and struggled through my description of its flight to freedom, and in fact for the remainder of the act. Naturally the total effect from the audience point of view was more risible than moving.

A FUNNY THING HAPPENED

to Harry Secombe..

I was due at the Windmill Theatre at 9.30 a.m. to perform my Army concert party act . . . The stage door keeper carefully scrutinised the letter I presented to him and sent me down the stone steps under the stage. The place was packed with hopeful auditionees of all kinds — singers nervously vocalising scales, conjurers practising card tricks with sweaty hands, and one gentleman in full Chinese make-up struggling with an enormous cabinet.

I went over to a short tubby man who had a list in his hand and gave him my name. He checked it against the names on his piece of paper and nodded briskly. 'You're on after the Chinese geezer,' he said in a gravelly voice.

'May I borrow a small table?' I asked tentatively. 'It's for my act.'

He returned with a small green felt card table and again told me who I followed. 'Be in the wings on time,' he said. 'They don't last long on there.'

Thoughtfully I began to prepare my props, first placing a sheet of newspaper on the table then putting on it the shaving brush, safety razor and folded towel. I filled my shaving mug at a tap in the toilet and began to lather up.

'You should have shaved before you came,' said the tubby man.

'This is my act,' I said in a small voice.

'Good God!' he said and walked away shaking his head.

An earnest young man in a blue striped suit came up to me and introduced himself. 'I'm Ronnie Bridges, the pianist. Have you any music you want played?'

I handed him a tattered song copy of 'Sweetheart'. 'I do it in two voices. The high one is Jeanette MacDonald and the low one is Nelson Eddy. When they're supposed to sing together I do a kind of yodel.'

'Yes, I see,' said the pianist slowly, taking in for the first time my shaving brush and the lather I was now vigorously applying to my face.

'This is the first part of the act,' I explained, splattering him with shaving soap on the 'p' of 'part'.

'What about play-on music? What tune would you like me to play on your entrance?'

'"I'm Just Wild About Harry" — because that's my name, Harry.'

'Very good. Very original. I think I can busk that.' He backed away smiling nervously.

'Thanks,' I said, applying more soap to the brush.

By this time I had cleared a corner for myself and some of the other hopefuls were eyeing me curiously, glad to have something to take their minds off the coming ordeal . . .

The Chinese magician in full Mandarin robes and make up wrestled his huge cabinet on stage. He put it in position and shuffled down front with his arms folded oriental fashion inside his sleeves.

'Velly good evening,' he began.

'There's no time for that,' said the voice from the stalls.

The Chinaman straightened up. 'No time for what, Mr. Van Damm?' he said anxiously in a heavy Geordie accent.

'All that cabinet nonsense. Can you do something simple?'

'Well, there's the disappearing coin trick. Flustered, the magician took a coin from a pocket in his voluminous robe and started doing a sleight of hand routine with it.

'Sorry,' said the dispassionate voice. 'Next.'

'Sod it,' said the Mandarin despairingly.

In the wings I had lathered myself into a frenzy watching the fate of my fellow victims, and when the tubby man, who turned out to be the stage manager, tapped me on the shoulder I raced on to the stage with my table. My one thought was to get the business over as quickly as possible and return to the safe clerical job in Baldwin's Colliery Office in Swansea — if they would have me back, that was.

'Everybody has to shave, except of course women and small children — but nobody shaves in exactly the same way. Take, for example, a small boy shaving for the first time . . .'

Before I knew where I was I had finished the shaving routine and was into the duet with myself. Ronnie Bridges gave me every possible assistance in spite of the fact that I was so hysterical that I over-rode every musical cue marked on the song copy. Once or twice I was vaguely aware of grunts from the stalls and I could only assume that the impresario was having a heart attack at my sheer effrontery.

I finished in a welter of flying soap suds from my soaked hair, as I threw my head back on the last note of 'Sweetheart'. I remained with my hands held high as if in surrender.

'Come and see me after the audition,' said the voice without a trace of expression.

I nodded dumbly and, picking up my table, slithered off stage.

In the wings a tall effeminate man stood facing me with his hands on his hips. 'You mucky thing,' he said. 'I've got to dance on that floor later on.'

'Sorry,' I said.

'I should think so,' he replied, flouncing off.

The stage manager grinned at me. 'You've upset him, and you might be working with him later on — he's in the resident show.'

'Do you think I've passed the audition then?' I was incredulous. I thought I had been told to stay behind so that I could be ticked off for wasting Van Damm's time.

'If he wants to see you after the audition that only means one thing. You're in.'

I began to tremble with delayed shock. What sort of money could I ask for? When would I be wanted? I assumed a Zombie-like stance. The stage manager moved me out of the way gently but firmly.

Ten minutes later in a clean shirt, but with soap still clinging to my hair and blocking my ears, I stood before Van Damm in his office.

'Very original turn,' said the distinguished-looking grey-haired man in the smart pin-striped suit. At his side Anne Mitelle, his personal assistant, smiled kindly at me. I stammered some self-deprecating remark.

'What money do you want?' he said looking into my eyes and not smiling.

'Ah, yes,' I floundered. I had no idea what to ask for. In the Army I had been getting three and sixpence a day for doing this same act, and I suddenly remembered an old pro telling me that if I asked a high enough figure I could always come down. What was the most astronomical figure I could think of? 'Twenty pounds a week.' The words came out in the same soprano register I used for Jeanette MacDonald.

'Right, done.' The impresario stood up and shook my hand. 'Miss Mitelle will draw up the contract. Good luck.'

Extract from 'Goon for Lunch' by Harry Secombe published by Michael Joseph Ltd.

to Arthur Askey..

During rehearsals, Mrs. Bromley Taylor decided to include a 'flying ballet'. Eventually they found somebody who apparently knew all the tricks and mechanics of 'flying', although he appeared with a very doubtful-looking set of equipment which seemed as if it had belonged to Grimaldi. The youngsters who played the Tempers (bad Tempers dressed in red, good Tempers in white) were between ten and fourteen years of age. Came dress rehearsal and they were strapped in their harnesses, the stage hands were given brief instructions as to which ropes they had to pull, and then the panic started. The kids were swung up into the air, some sideways, some upside down, and they spun around, banging into each other, some just off the floor, others right up in the flies. Most of them were crying but the orchestra played on. The ballet was supposed to be brought to an end by the appearance of the King of Temperland. He was a large six-foot-three bass and his entrance was to be effected by his standing on a step-ladder in the wings and then, on cue, gliding on his wire to the centre of the stage. He jumped off the ladder as instructed, and fell flat on his face, while the two men holding on to the rope shot about ten feet in the air. Needless to say, the flying ballet was cut.

Another member of the cast of another panto was 'Monsewer Eddie Gray'.

He was always ready for a practical joke. I remember on one occasion coming off the North Pier, Blackpool, after a show, when Eddie stopped by a pillar box. It was midday and the usual lunchtime crowds were milling around. Eddie went up to the pillar box and began shouting through the letter slot: 'Well how did you get in there in the first place?' He then put his ear to the slot and carried on a bizarre conversation, finishing with, 'Well don't panic. I'll fetch the fire brigade!' By the time we moved off there were about five hundred people waiting to see the rescue.

Excerpt from 'Before Your Very Eyes' by Arthur Askey published by The Woburn Press

After Dinner Mints II.

Reading Robert Henriques' autobiographical novel, *The Commander,* I find a reference to General Adrian Carton de Wiart, that gallant soldier who won the V.C. and lost an eye and an arm. Predictably, a man of his courage would not allow these disabilities to stop him from indulging in his favourite sport, shooting. His gun, on such occasions, was strapped to his remaining arm, so that he had to rely on his Batman to load – and indeed do all else, manually, that could not be done with the metal hook which replaced the war hero's lost hand.

Out on the moors one day, ahead of his party, the General felt a call of nature and prudently retired behind a gorse bush, with his Batman – as usual – to assist him. The Batman seemed to be taking his time. 'Hurry up, man!' said the General, 'the ladies will be here in a minute.'

'Very sorry, sir,' apologised the Batman, 'I can't find it.'

'Damn it all man?' said the General testily, '*You* had it last.'

At the last General Election a local worthy offered to provide transport to and from the polling stations. The front door of a small house, on which she had called, was opened by a woman to whom she explained the purpose of her visit.

'Well,' said the woman doubtfully, 'It all depends which party you're from, dunnit? I mean to say, I'm Labour, myself see?'

The good lady explained that her sevices were non-partisan and that she would be pleased to take her. The woman seemed still to be in doubt. 'I better go and have a word with my friend. She lives with me, see, and she's Conservative.'

Mrs H. said she'd wait, relieved no doubt that the votes would cancel each other out. It was some minutes before the woman returned to the front door. 'I made a mistake,' she said, 'My friend's just told me. *I'm* Conservative, see? It's *her* that's Labour.'

*MONJA DANISCHEWSKY**

It is related of Oscar Wilde that he was standing aloof at a party when his hostess came up to him and asked him anxiously, "Are you enjoying yourself, Mr. Wilde?"

"Yes, I am," he said, "There is nothing else here to enjoy."

Two Russian workers, Ivan and Boris, were discussing the possibility of going to work at a construction site in Siberia. They had been told that conditions at the site were excellent and that wages were good. However, rather than both of them taking the risk of finding matters less than good, it was agreed that one would go and write to the other.

Ivan lost the toss of the coin and agreed to go. They then discussed the difficulty of the letter which would be sent describing conditions. Ivan said he was not anxious to send a letter saying that conditions were bad and it was agreed that if the letter were written in blue ink it would be true. On the other hand, if it were in red ink it needed to be taken with a large pinch of salt.

Some weeks passed and the letter arrived. Boris observed it was in blue ink and read it with interest.

"Dear Boris,

The conditions here are very good, safety, health and welfare are provided for. The living accommodation is excellent. The supermarket has everything. Fresh bread daily, sausages, pork and every kind of meat. Clothing can be bought cheaply. In fact, I can buy many more things here than in Moscow. There seems to be only one shortage. Unfortunately I cannot buy red ink!!"

Excerpt from 'Out Of My Mind' by Monja Danischewsky published by Michael Joseph Ltd.

VIEWS OF THE WORLD

MAN UPSET OVER TEA AND CRUMPET

"Although I would not describe myself as an enthusiast for censorship," said Mr Thomas Gain, a Northumbrian greengrocer, "I was anxious about my tea. The intolerable delay drove me to a frenzy."

Mr Gain was describing a series of events that led to his being charged with an indecent assault against Miss Maureen Welter, a secretary, while they were on a free church coach tour of the Lake District.

"After our picnic lunch," Mr Gain said, "Miss Welter insisted upon bathing in Derwent water in her underclothes. Our minister, Dr Frilly, warned her that this could incite the coach-driver, and at least three of her fellow tourists asked her not to jump up and down in front of him while shouting "Springtime! Springtime!"

"We had reboarded the coach and were looking forward to tea at *Hellvellyn Heights* when the coach driver turned into a lane and, nodding towards Miss Welter, clambered out and onto the nearside bank.

"After a few minutes it became obvious to the tour that the couple were making love. Most people chose to ignore them; but when they went at it for the third time, I saw red."

According to Miss Welter, Mr Gain left the coach, approached her at the run, and sank his teeth into her buttocks. She was in pain for several days. "And permanently scarred."

Miss Welter was fined £25 and Mr Gain was ordered to pay both of their costs.

Soccer Hooligan

During an action for divorce the judge asked the wife for an example of her husband's behaviour. She replied: "Last year Harry asked me if I had anything to discuss before the football season began."

Tickled Pink

As part of a serious attempt to resurrect their former passion, Mrs Magda Friederich of Munich purchased a Pinkie-Winkie See-thru Babydoll Nightie with which she hoped to arouse her husband on the night of their 27th wedding anniversary.

Mr Friederich, a dentist, showed his appreciation. Thereafter, his wife developed an almost sacred attachment to the colour pink.

The following day she bought a two-piece pink suit with matching suit and gloves; to this costume she added a pink hat and handbag; soon afterwards she limited herself to pink make-up.

At first Mr Friederich said nothing; but when his wife introduced pink wallpaper, pink carpets, pink napkins, tablecloths, dishclothes, curtains, towels, chairs, electric light bulbs, and would tune the colour set to an overall pinkish glow, he decided to speak.

Mrs Friederich would not be deterred. She responded to his complaints by buying pink pots and pans, and, late one night, she dyed her own and her husband's clothes Petunia Roseblush.

Her final gesture was to bring the pink into his surgery where she dyed the surgical chair Musk Blush Winter Poppy.

"I'm just mad about it," she said. "I'm going to be divorced in pink."

Secret Recipe

Madame Ivy Cannon, a charwoman employed at The Ministry of War, has been given two years' imprisonment plus a £500 fine for covering her jampots with top secret military documents.

WHERE THERE'S A WILL THERE'S A WAY

Forging Howard Hughes's will is turning into something of a national sport. Nine more purported wills were delivered to the Las Vegas courthouse in the lastest post, bringing the total to 17.

Mr George Holt, the District Attorney, seeking to curb this minor growth industry, announced he will prosecute anyone suspected of forging the last testament of the multi-millionaire recluse.

One version named Richard Robard Hughes as sole beneficiary of the £1,100 million estate. He has said he is Hughes's illegitimate son.

He also made the unlikely claim he could communicate with Hughes via a radio implanted in his head that he switched on by a flick of the tongue. An X-ray showed what appeared to be a car fuse stuck in his ear.

Going for a Song

Among a troup of entertainers visiting Parramatta Gaol, near Sydney (Australia), was 23-year-old Sharon Hamilton, a singer of uplifting folk melodies.

Hardly had she finished the opening stanza of "We shall Overcome", when Leonard Lawson, a rapist, leapt onto the stand and, holding a knife to Miss Hamilton's throat, asked the audience to leave the room as he wanted to be alone with her.

Two of his fellow prisoners overpowered him. Miss Hamilton had five stitches in her throat.

Fantastic journey

When Mrs Alva Mays of Muleshoe, Texas, heard that her sister-in-law had been injured in a freeway pileup, she set off by car to see her.

Entering the Santa Monica Freeway at 9.18 a.m, she began a journey of nearly 1,000 freeway miles that included 16 unsuccessful negotiations of the downtown Los Angeles interchange, a night in Bakersville, six traffic violations for both fast and slow driving, 12 hours trapped in dense fog on the Oceanside overpass, and an extensive survey of nine separate freeway systems from which she emerged three days later by driving through the barrier protecting the new four mile extension of the Garden Grove Freeway, where she crashed into the crowd attending the opening ceremony.

Room with a View

Twelve months after they had installed a television set in her home, a firm of electrical suppliers received a call from their customer in the course of which she explained that the set was keeping her awake at night.

When an engineer arrived at the lady's house he asked her if she had tried turning it off.

"I did not know that you could switch it off," she said. "The picture is excellent, but after a year I do feel in need of a rest."

Groan Groan!

What goes up bell ropes and is wrapped in a polythene bag? The lunchpack of Notre Dame.

It has recently been discovered that Wales is sinking into the sea—due to the many leeks in the ground.

Dolphins are so intelligent that within only a few weeks of being in captivity they can train a man to stand on the very edge of their pool and throw them fish three times a day.

The plan to wrap all meat pies in tin has been foiled.

The Mediterranean and Red Seas are joined by the Sewage Canal.

A strawberry was reported today to be in a bit of a jam.

In court this morning was a young man accused of peddling drugs. He said he had left his bicycle at home.

'That's a lovely bulldog you've got there.'
'No, it's not a bulldog—it was chasing a cat and ran into a wall.'

A man tried to stab me early this evening. He was a man after my own heart.

A man who beat his carpet to death a few hours ago is soon expected to be charged with matricide.

Speaking about the droppings of pigeons in the town, a council official said: 'We must try not to dodge the issue.'

What is the difference between unlawful and illegal? Unlawful is against the law. Illegal is a sick bird.

What is the difference between a buffalo and a bison? Ever tried to wash your hands in a buffalo?

What do you put on a pig with a sore nose? Oinkment.

Owing to a strike at the meteorological office, there will be no weather tomorrow.

What is smooth, round and green and conquered the world? Alexander the Grape!

An inflatable rubber lilo collapsed and died today at its South Harrow home.

A hymn has recently been dedicated to a Birmingham corset factory. It is 'All Is Safely Gathered In.'

Yesterday, five hundred men walked out of a steel mill while it was still in operation. A Union spokesman said they had to strike while the iron was hot.

Why does a giraffe have such a long neck? Because it can't stand the smell of its feet

'Waiter! This coffee tastes like mud.'
'Well, sir, it was ground only ten minutes ago.'

It was reported this afternoon that a man in Cornwall was partially electrocuted. After his recovery the man said: 'It came as something of a shock.'

RING DEM BELLS

Now who's going to say grace?

Once you latch on to the fact that it's not the belief you're making fun of, but the people who practise — and preach — it, then religion and laughter seem alright. How else, really, can you look at the stuffed-shirt solemnity we seem to think appropriate for church and chapel coupled with the laughable way we all usually carry on? Like the time a country church council was discussing the urgent need for an altar rail for the older churchgoers because "we don't want them falling forward and perhaps dying of shock" and the vicar, quick as a flash, cutting in "oh but we're insured against that". Or the small girl who complained at Sunday School that the Ten Commandments didn't seem to help her much, they just put ideas into her head. Or the local drunk who, having staggered into the church after closing time for a quiet snooze, woke past midnight in the pitch dark to find himself firmly locked in, groped his way via the font to the bell ropes — and shattered the sleeping village with a frantic clang-dang of let-me-out bell-ringing that sent the rooks sky high and the sexton reaching for his gun.

And anyway — to up-end the old if-God-intended-us-to-fly-he'd-have-given-us-wings routine — **I'd** *say that if He hadn't intended us to laugh, He wouldn't have given us a sense of humour.*

K.B.

Two sailors were going home on leave after a rough time in the Cod War. Arriving at Invergordon to go on their leave they got into a train and found themselves sharing a compartment with a parson.
After the train moved off a little, one sailor says to the other, "What are you going to do with your leave Jack?"
"I am going to get drunk on beer every night. That's my hobby. How about you?' The other sailor says, "Girls are my hobby. I am going to see a different one every night and have a marvellous time."
The train moves on. One sailor looks at the paper and on reading it says to his friend, "What's lumbago, Jack?"
"I don't know—ask the parson," was the reply.
So the sailor says, "What's lumbago, sir?"
As the parson was annoyed at the way they had been talking, he replied, "Lumbago, my man, is a very painful disease, due to drinking beer and going out with women. Why do you ask?"
"It's nothing, gun'nor—it just says in the paper here that the Bishop of London has got it."

Two brothers, members of a very ancient and noble English family, hated each other all through school and college. After graduating, they went their separate ways, one into the navy and the other into the church. In the course of time, the first brother became an admiral, and the second a bishop.

They didn't meet for many years, but one day by chance, they spotted each other on the platform at Waterloo. The admiral was in full dress uniform, having just come from an investiture at Buckingham Palace; the bishop, grown fat and pot-bellied, was attired in his usual walking-out dress of frock and gaiters.

They stared at each other for a moment, pretending not to recognise each other, then finally the bishop said, 'I say, stationmaster — is the 6.15 for Bournemouth running on time this evening?'

'Yes, madam' replied the admiral, 'but is it wise to travel in your condition?'

When it came to Church Parades the Services recognised only Church of England, Roman Catholics and the all-embracing Other Denominations. The first two sects provided by far the largest contingents but there were always some 'odds and sods'. A certain Warrant Officer found this out early in his long service and whenever a man claimed to be a member of some way-out sect he honoured the service practice of giving him some unpleasant job to discourage him from dodging the parade under false pretences.

On one occasion, when the varous contingents had marched off, there was still one man waiting. The WO approached him grimly, 'Are you Jewish?' he asked. 'No sir,' replied the man. 'I'm a member of the Society of Friends.' 'The *what?*' The airman made it easier for the WO. 'A Quaker sir.' This was a new one on the WO but he was equal to it and he told the odd man out to go and clean the latrines. The following Sunday the WO's eagle eye spotted the Quaker lad among the C of Es and he went to stand in front of him with a vicious grin 'Got converted eh?' 'No sir,' replied the Member of the Society of Friends. 'I'm still a Quaker but I don't like the place they have to worship in.'

'If I can get really addicted, it will be something new to give up—!'

from 'The Book Of The Monk' by Hugh Burnett published by Merlin Press Ltd.

A businessman, who needed a couple of million pounds to clinch a deal, decided to go to church and pray for the money. By chance he knelt next to a man who was praying aloud for £25 to pay an urgent debt. The businessman took out his wallet and pressed the £25 into the other man's hand. Overjoyed, the man got up and left the church. The businessman closed his eyes again, and prayed "And now, Lord, may I have your undivided attention."

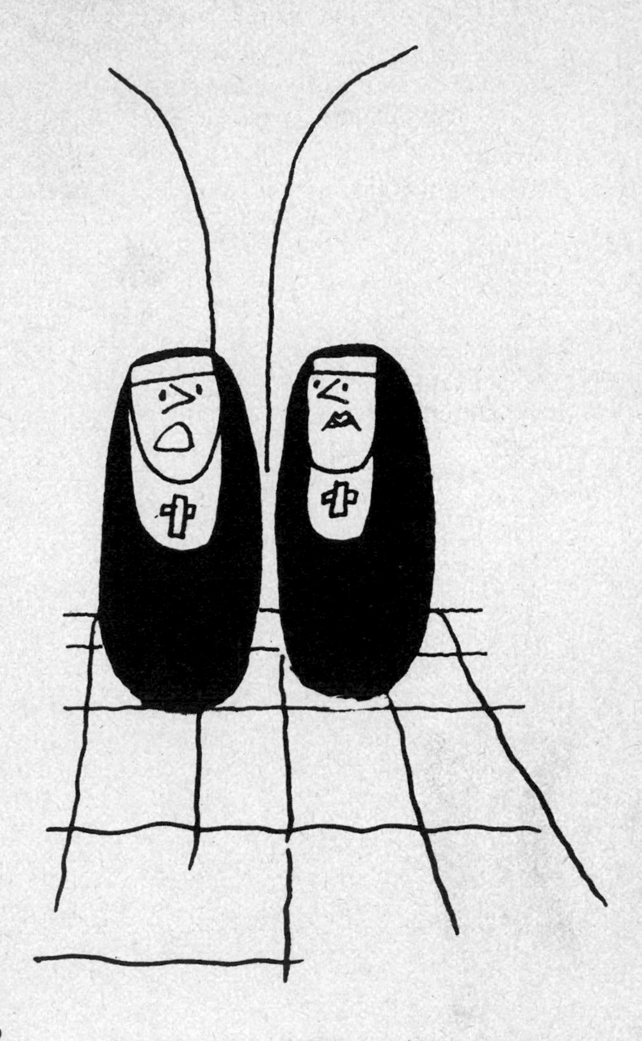

'My knees are killing me.'

'Three men, sir; and probably in disguise!'

Four ministers of different denominations frequently met for fellowship. One day they decided to help one another by confessing sins while the others listened sympathetically.

The Episcopalian rector began by admitting his pet sin was drinking. The Methodist declared his problem was with gambling. The Presbyterian admitted that he smoked behind the backs of his church members. After a long pause, one of the men prodded the Baptist minister and said, "What about you, brother? Or don't you have a pet sin?"

"I have one, but I don't think you'd want to hear it," said the Baptist.

"Yes, we would," chorused the other three. "We insist."

"Well, my pet sin," said the Baptist, "is gossip — and I can hardly wait to get to a telephone."

Cartoons from 'More Barnabus' by Graham Jeffery published by Wolfe Publishing Ltd.

IT PAYS TO ADVERTISE. . . . .

WHERE YOU GO IN THE HEREAFTER DEPENDS ON WHAT YOU GO AFTER DOWN HERE.

COME IN AND HAVE YOUR FAITH LIFTED.

WE HOLD SIT-IN DEMONSTRATIONS EVERY SUNDAY MORNING.

YOU CAN'T TAKE IT WITH YOU, BUT YOU CAN SEND IT ON AHEAD.

DON'T EXPECT A THOUSAND-POUND ANSWER TO A TEN-PENNY PRAYER.

GIVE IN ACCORDANCE WITH WHAT YOU REPORTED ON YOUR INCOME TAX.

ASK ABOUT OUR PRAY-AS-YOU-GO PLAN.

IF YOU HAVE TROUBLES, COME IN AND TELL US ABOUT THEM. IF NOT, COME IN AND TELL US HOW YOU DO IT.

DAILY SERVICES. COME EARLY IF YOU WANT A BACK SEAT.

PRAY UP IN ADVANCE.

GIVE UP POT FOR LENT.

COME IN AND LET US PREPARE YOU FOR YOUR FINALS.

. . . . . ON CHURCH NOTICEBOARDS?

Amin dies, and ascends to heaven. St. Peter refuses him entry, and sends him down to hell.

The next day, St. Peter is woken early by a great clamour outside his window. Looking out, he sees a huge crowd of devils, all demanding political asylum.

A little boy, who was the only child of parents who lived on the north side of the Ulster/Eire border, was asked to go for a picnic with a little girl, who was the only child of parents on the south side of the border.

It was a sunny, hot July day and they picnicked by a river. The children took all their clothes off and played in the water.

When the little boy got home his mother said to him "Johnny, was it interesting?" and he replied, "Yes, Mummy, it was fascinating. I never knew before what a big difference there is between Protestants and Catholics."

A young Irish girl goes to church for confession, and says to the priest, "Oh Father, Father, I have sinned grieviously. On Monday night I slept with Sean. On Tuesday night I slept with Patrick, and on Wednesday night I slept with Patrick, and on Wednesday night I slept with Mick. Oh Father, Father, what shall I do?"

"My child, my child," replied the priest, "go home and squeeze the juice from a whole lemon and drink it."

"Oh Father, Father will this purge me of my sin?" she asked.

"No child, but it will take the smile off your face."

'Father, I want you to meet Mother.'

Nicholas Bentley 'How Can You Bear To Be Human' published by Andre Deutsch Ltd.

Tommy Cooper

JUST LIKE THAT . . .

The fact is, I've always wanted to write something. Everyone does. You've only got to go into a public place and you can see what struggling would-be writers are trying to get out. For example, on one wall I saw written, 'Smoking stunts your growth'. Below it, about two feet off the ground, someone else had written, 'Now he tells me.'

The fact is, there are poems and all sorts of interesting items, complete with illustrations, to be found on walls. This goes to show how many budding authors there are and I know they really appreciate their readers. I once saw a beautifully written notice on the wall of a little place beneath Tottenham Court Road which simply said, 'We wish all our readers a Merry Christmas.' I thought it charming. It expressed the depth of feeling that exists between writer and reader.

Anyway, I gave a good deal of thought to this writing business. I thought, what can I write about? I mean, I've been around. I've tried my hand at all sorts of jobs. You wouldn't believe it. For instance, I once had a job painting the white lines down roadways. I packed it in before I went round the bend. Then there was a job where I took things easy and the next job where they locked everything away.

Should I write about the funny people I've met in my time? Like the cat burglar. He stole hundreds of cats. He was politically motivated. He was a Meeowist. And what about the Siamese Twins who held up a bank? They didn't wear stocking masks. They shared a pair of tights. I knew a cannibal who was fond of titbits and his brother who had been influenced by Catholic missionaries: on Fridays he only ate fishermen. I once fought a boxer with an ingrowing nose and ingrowing ears. I lived next door to a van driver who was always smashing into the backs of vans. He was a vandal. Nobody wanted any truck with him.

Now, I've been interested in jokes and tricks all my life. I was always reading books about jokes and tricks. At school, my teacher said I was a very tricky customer and that she thought my schoolwork was just a big joke. I once knew a man who did tricks with saucers. He was a sorcerer. Another chap I knew did tricks with jugs. He was a juggler. Then it came to me in a flash. It was a flash in the pen. I would write about jokes and tricks. After all, that is what life is all about when you think about it. So that's what I've done.

Anyone can be the life and soul of a party once they can perform a few baffling tricks. The tricks I'm going to tell you about are very baffling to be sure. They even baffle me.

Now, when doing tricks make sure your audience is awake, but not too wide awake or you might get one of those know-it-all Charlies giving the game away. Do a bit of the old patter; the old friendly chatter. It helps take people's mind off exactly how you are doing what. Wave a bamboo cane about. It will bamboozle your audience. Do a bit of what they call 'business' in the business. A little horseplay, you know: I saw this poor little horse. It was starving. It had no fodder. What is worse, it had no modder.

Now here's an easy trick for starters. It usually makes a big impression. It's a variation of the old sawing a lady in half bit. So you'll need a saw. Place your hand down on a table and tell your audience you are going to saw off a finger. Saw off a finger. Then hold up your hand and show you still have five fingers. *Wait! As you were! Hang about!* I should have mentioned that to do this trick successfully you need to be six fingered to start with.

We had a man in the office once. He ate the staples from the stapling machine. He said it was his staple diet. I knew a sailor who was always blubbering. He was a wailer. I merely mention this in passing while I'm thinking of my next trick. I knew a Chinese once. He struck himself with a chopper. He committed chop-sueycide. And talking of Chinese, here's a Chinese trick. I got it from an old opium smoker. It's called the Chinese smoke trick.

You take two glasses. Place one on top of the other (see sketch) and cover quickly with a hand towel. Tell your audience you are going to blow smoke through the towel and into the glasses.

Someone might say, 'So what?' Ignore him, her or it. Roll up a tissue and light in. Blow out the flame and as the paper smoulders blow the smoke towards the towel. Now say the magic phrase which is what the fiddler said to the flautist, 'Up your flute!' Remove the towel from the glasses. The glasses are full of smoke. Hold a glass in each hand and watch the faces of your audience as they watch your smoke.

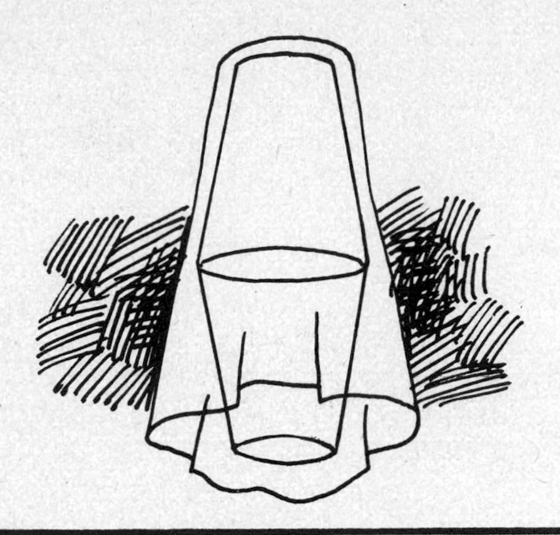

How is it done? I'm not sure. Hang about. Yes. It's done like this. In one glass you put a drop of household ammonia. In the other a drop of hydrochloric acid. Keep the glasses covered until you use them. When the chemicals combine you get the smoke effect. You have to be quick and slick for this trick like I am, but a word of warning: hydrochloric acid is corrosive so don't go throwing it about.

Here's a quick trick. Throw a 10p coin into the air and drill it before it hits the ground. All you have to do is use a 10p shooter.

There was a man who couldn't resist driving away cars. The judge asked him why he did it. He said he was just motorvated. He went to prison. He was put in a cell used for beating up prisoners. It was known as the hiding place. It was so small it was hard to do a good stretch. The judge was named Smith. He was one of the great Scottish clan of Smiths. The Loch Smiths. Once, during a murder trial, he released the accused and sent the whole jury to the gallows. It was a hung jury.

Excerpt from 'Just Like That' published by Jupiter Books Ltd.

From The Roy Hudd Joke Book

published by Wolfe Publishing Ltd.

ON HOLIDAY

The landlay's husband gave us the bill at the end of the week. It said 'extras, five pounds.'

I said: 'What's this "extra five pounds"?'

He said: 'That's for the use of the cruet.'

I said: 'I never used the cruet.'

He said: 'It was there if you wanted to.'

I gave him the money less the fiver and said: 'Sorry about that fiver, that's for kissing my wife.'

He said: 'I never kissed your wife.'

I said: 'It was there if you wanted to.'

What a week we had it only rained twice—once for three days and once for four.

HIS FAMILY

My mother-in-law's got a lovely little personality. A rag and bone man called the other day and said: 'Have you got any empty beer bottles?'

She said: 'Do I look as if I drink beer?'

'Well, got any empty vinegar bottles, then?'

Dad used to think marriage was like a self service cafe. You get exactly what you want – and as soon as you see what the other fella's got you want a bit of that an' all.

When I was a baby, what I really dreaded was dad changing my nappy. You see, he was a hand grenade instructor at the time, and through force of habit he used to pull out the pin, count five, then lob me over the nearest wall.

My wife's mad on frozen food. She gave me so much of it, that I had to go to the doctor with stomach trouble. I said: 'What is it, doc? Ulcers?'

'No, frostbite.'

The Daily Blooper

Hunter Robert Coury, aged 23, was in hospital in Mesa, Arizona, yesterday, after accidentally shooting himself in the leg with his pistol — and then shooting himself in the other leg when he fired the gun to summon aid.

Daily Express

MR GEORGE DOBBS, of Chertsey, is very proud of the fact that he walked 50 miles on a sausage sandwich at the weekend.

Staines and Egham News

Wrap poison bottles in sandpaper and fasten with scotch tape or a rubber band. If there are children in the house, lock them in a small metal box.

Philadelphia Record

The constable now preferred a further charge against the two girls of stealing a carving knife, a fork, and two ornamental judges which he found on the top of a wardrobe in the hotel bedroom.

Dublin Evening Mail

POLICE FOUND SAFE UNDER BLANKET

Headline in Gloucestershire Echo

A basement flat comprising three rooms, kitchen, bathroom, outside WC (at present occupied by owner).

House Agents' leaflet

BOLOGNA, December 13. *Umberto Montanari was unable to get rid of a mouse which chewed holes in his car's carpet, so he put a pot of water inside the vehicle and dropped a block of carbide into it. The method succeeded. An explosion destroyed the mouse—and the car.*

Reuter

We have often in the past had Wimbledon wobbles with nervy players so shaky that their boobs have sometimes made park club players blush.

Scottish Daily Express

A letter addressed to 'Degenerate Bawd' in London has been correctly deciphered by the Post Office as being intended for the Central Electricity Generating Board, according to the February issue of *Power News.*

Evening Standard

A second-hand car dealer in Connecticut has learned that it doesn't pay to use slang in advertising. He advertised a 1962 Pontiac for '1,395 bananas' (slang for dollars). When a housewife offered him 25 bananas on deposit, he refused to accept it. The housewife sued, alleged false advertising, and won her case. She presented the dealer with the balance of bananas and drove the car away.

SUNDAY TIMES

From the Radio Times

1.30 *Colour: New series*
Watch with Mother
Mr Benn
Every week Mr Benn dresses-up and finds himself in a new adventure.

This summer the Graham family—father, mother and teenage daughter—will move into the bungalow which they have planned and built themselves from books borrowed from their local library.

Sunday Express

Police surmised that the *widow* had been pried open with a crowbar and entry made by means of a stepladder found near the scene.

Declared the Rev. Lord Soper: "I am at this moment responsible for 14 pregnant girls in a hostel . . ."

Daily Express

Dr S— is associated with societies for the prohibition of cruel sports, recorder playing and Welsh folk songs.

Yorkshire Post

'I GOT something off my chest today that's been hanging over my head for sometime. That's behind me now, thank goodness.'

Film star on B.B.C. interview

The first essential in the treatment of burns is that the patient should be removed from the fire.

First Aid Manual

THE CREWE committee has arranged to apply the vaccine to 20 calves in October and three months later five or six more will be inoculated. Later, some of both lots will be killed for the post-mortem examination, and if it is likely to prove beneficial, human beings will be similarly treated.

Austrialian paper

MEDICAL MADNESS

GEORGE, IF YOU THINK IT'S CONTAGIOUS – DON'T BRING GRAPES!

We all know by now that it's murder looking up anything in those home medicine books. All you want is a simple cure for warts but on the way through to the W section you accidentally read so many vividly described and hideous symptoms that you've got the lot before you even get to M, and why worry about warts, it's obviously your last will and testament you should be thinking about.

Books of short sharp medical facts aren't a whole lot better. "Fifty million of your cells will have died" one just told me "while you've been reading this sentence." No wonder I've been feeling a bit frail since I finished that novel the other day. And of course the fact that "your brain uses as much power as a 10-watt electric bulb" would explain why I felt a bit dim too. To crown it all (as if advertisements didn't go on enough already about bad breath and pimples) I now learn that I "constantly shed particles of skin, amounting to one entire outer layer every 28 days." Can it really be that I move through the world trailing not clouds of glory or even unacceptable personal odours, but a thin persistent mist of skin particles?

Oh doctor, doctor, do not tell me more.

K.B.

Twice Daily

A Swedish psychoanalyst wrote extensively on the importance of charging high fees. He argued that in this way the analyst presents himself as a forthright individual who dares to be honest about money and is thus worthy of emulation. The fat fee was also an excellent outlet for the neurotic feelings of the masochistic patient, and a large bill did away with any potentially damaging 'humiliating sense of gratitude'.

When a general retired as head of the US Chemical Corps he visited each installation to say goodbye to his men. At one base an elaborate demonstration was staged in which several thousand guinea pigs were satisfactorily exterminated with nerve gas. Impressed, the general remarked: 'Now we know what to do if we ever go to war against guinea pigs'.

A man went to a doctor because he was feeling ill and thought he was going to die. "What can I do to get well and live to a ripe old age?" he asked. The doctor told him: "Give up drink, tobacco and women and you will live to be a hundred". "Will I really live to be a hundred?" eagerly asked the patient. "No", replied the doctor, "but it will seem like it".

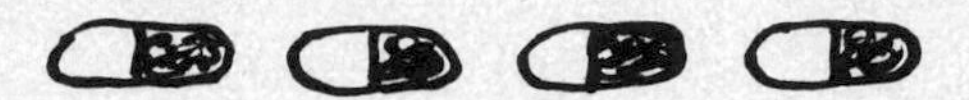

British blood is growing hotter. According to the Polish daily *Express Posnanski* in 1968: 'Because of the increased sexuality of the Anglo-Saxons, it was proved possible to exceed our planned output of mistletoe.'

A group of schoolboys nominated a leading dermatologist 'sportsman of the year' for having written that 'skin diseases in civilised countries due to excessive washing are commoner than those attributed to dirt'.

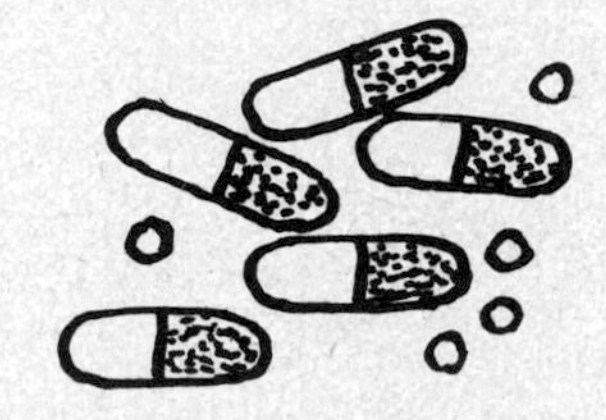

It was thought indecent for Chinese women to undress in front of doctors, who therefore had to provide ivory statuettes on which the ladies could point out where they felt unwell.

Diligent research quickly produced an effective contraceptive pill for men, but it turned users' eyeballs pink if they drank alcohol. Research continues.

The difference between a lawyer and a surgeon is that a lawyer concerned with leaving nothing out and a surgeon is concerned with leaving nothing in.

'So that's why you keep asking for more grapes' Gilbert!

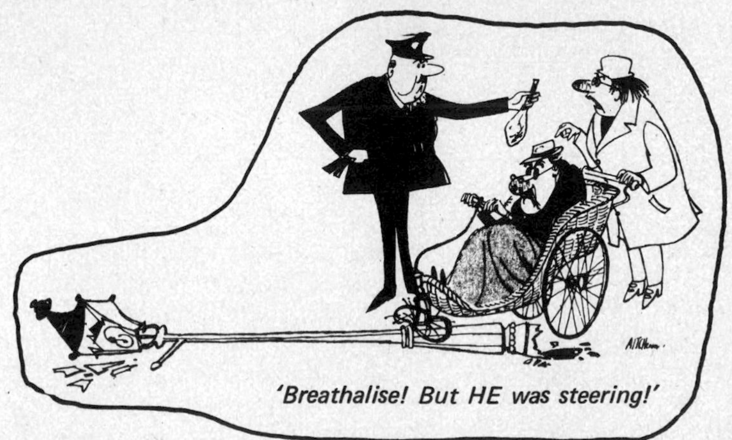

'Breathalise! But HE was steering!'

Your Teeth in Their Hands

by ALAN COREN

According to a report commissioned by the General Dental Practitioners' Association, the average dentist is "oppressed by health, ageing, status ambiguity, social paranoia and social isolation, and has become neurotic over his inability to achieve the same social recognition as the medical practitioner". What dentistry requires, clearly, is a new Image, a Folk Myth, a Kildare or Ben Casey—in short, a Great Romantic Hero.

The Story So Far: When tall, azure-eyed, blond-haired undergrad Lord Dunromin flees Oxford two days after stroking his boat to victory, London's social world is flung into baffled misery. His unutterably beautiful fiancée, model girl Princess Doreen of Labia, receives a note from the West London Air Terminal saying that Dunromin has decided to shoulder the blame for his guardsman brother's indiscretions in St. James's Park, and leave England forever. Relinquishing his title, he joins the French Foreign Legion as plain Garth Genesis, and is immediately posted to the immeasurably disgusting Fort Zinderneuf, deep in the Sahara. The camp dentist has contracted *le cafard* and pliered himself to death, and the morale of the men is exceeding low: racked by caries, halitosis, gingivitis and Bedouin tongue-acne, they are ill-equipped to defend themselves against the hordes of crazed Touaregs who, fitted out with Oxfam dentures and Czech machine-guns, are preparing for their final assault on the garrison. But they have reckoned without Garth Genesis, whose enormous (yet amazingly witty) brain has applied itself to the task of learning the dentist's art: within days, aided only by a tawny, half-naked beauty from Lille (who called at the fort to sell vacuum-cleaners), Garth completely re-establishes dental hygiene among the men, working through the night by the dim light of a burning prisoner to fill holes, extract deficient molars, build sturdy bridgework until the regiment's teeth are the pride of the Legion. After the Touaregs are overwhelmingly defeated, Garth Genesis is awarded the Croix de Guerre, the Legion d'Honneur, and the B.D.S. and bar. By this time, his brother has confessed his crimes and opened fourteen male boutiques on the proceeds, whereupon Garth Genesis, after saving an upper Number Four of a visiting dignitary close to de Gaulle, is given an honourable discharge. He returns to England and a knighthood for services to Anglo-French relations, and sets up a surgery in Wimpole Street. Soon afterwards, however, a third cousin of the Queen for whom he has been designing a set of evening teeth and matching ear-rings, falls hopelessly in love with him and leaves her husband. *NOW READ ON:*

The Hon. Fenella Strume-Clavering's lovelorn eyes gazed down, intoxicated, as Garth Genesis's lithe fingers probed and caressed the dark, secret places of her mouth. They were the fingers of a dentist: strong, lean, tanned. Virile. Her heart pounded.

"Spit," he said.

She turned her exquisite head, bent over the bowl, unable to spit; a single tear rolled down her nose and splashed against the immaculate porcelain.

"You realise, madame," said Genesis levelly, "that there is absolutely nothing wrong with your teeth?"

She looked away from his unfathomable blue eyes.

"Yes," she whispered. "I know. But I had to come. I had——"

A bell tinkled, and Genesis sprang across to the instrument in one bound with the easy power of a panther trained to answer telephones. He listened, his fine brow furrowing.

"I'll be right over. Do nothing till I arrive."

He replaced the receiver, and turned once more to his ravishing patient.

"That was the Chief Commissioner," he said. "There's a chap at the top of the Millbank Tower threatening to throw himself off. I have to go."

Their eyes met for an enigmatic instant, and she flashed him a brave smile which he had done so much to create. Not for nothing was he known throughout the civilised world as the Benvenuto Cellini of the platinum inlay. He turned on a handshod heel and, in a whiff of lingering halothane, was gone.

* * *

A gale was shrieking round the roof, as Garth Genesis leapt from the service elevator: only for a second did he allow himself to glance down at the minuscle details of London, four hundred teetering feet below. Then, with a cry of "Let me through, I'm a dentist!" he plunged into the mass of doctors, archbishops, psychiatrists, journalists and back-bench politicians, all of whom instantly fell back reverently to let him pass. Beyond, at the very edge of the overhang, a man instantly recognisable as a TV personality loved by millions hovered between life and pavement. At the sight of Genesis, the matinée idol face broke into a wretched smile: the crowd gasped. Within the famous mouth, the rotted teeth hung like tiny salamis in some toytown delicatessen. "My career is at an end!" moaned the star; but a strong hand flew out to save and comfort. "Nonsense!" cried the great dentist. "Merely a case of arc-light rot. Put yourself in my hands: together we shall save you for posterity!" Weeping, the star stepped slowly back into the land of the living, and, as swiftly as he had come, Garth Genesis left once more. Behind him, the gale plucked the cheers from the mouths of tycoons and clerics and scattered them across a grateful land.

* * *

"Gargle, please!"

The Hon. Fenella Strume-Clavering dribbled miserably into the bowl, while her delectable tongue nudged numbly at the gap left by a vanished tooth. It had been a perfectly good canine, and only a fit of wild hysterics on her part had finally persuaded Genesis to extract it for what he had managed to convince himself were psychological reasons. For her, it had not seemed too high a price to pay for one more fleeting visit. She looked up at him with moist eyes.

"I hag leg my hugban!" she cried.

"Please try not to talk," he said gently.

"You doe uggertag!" shrieked the Hon. Fenella. "I hag leg my hugban!"

The great dentist frowned.

"You have left your husband?"

"Yeg!"

He smiled, and his splendid eyebrows rippled deliciously.

"It's merely the effect of the anaesthetic, dear lady," he said. "You'll feel perfectly all right in an hour or so."

Whereupon he bowed, left her in the care of his lovely nurse, and went to keep an appointment with the Prime Minister.

* * *

"Frankly and freely," said the Prime Minister, "and I do mean that sincerely, I find myself, as we all of us do, sometimes — I'm sure you yourself do — faced with something of a problem. It's a problem in which we all have a share, it's a problem I know we can lick if we just set aside our little personal differences for a short while, and pull together in this great — and I do mean great, I mean it most sincerely — this great country of ours. Frankly, fearlessly, honestly——"

"What exactly is the problem, Prime Minister?" said Garth Genesis, from his comfortable fauteuil opposite the throne.

"It's my smile," said the PM.

"Your smile?"

"It's been a good smile, I won't deny that," said the PM. "It's been frank, and fearless, and honest, and sincere for a good three years now, and I don't have to tell you what a strain that puts on the cheeks."

"The burdens of office, Prime Minister."

"Quite. But now, as we move together into the darkening storm, and the shadow of unemployment falls across this great country and my salary, I feel I need something a little special. Something noble. Saintly, almost."

Garth Genesis stood up and handed the PM his hand-tooled pattern book, indicating a couple of possible designs. The Prime Minister's tiny eyes lit up.

"Those!" he cried.

"Hi!"

"The doctor told him to take his temperature in the back passage"

"Impeccable, Prime Minister!" said Garth Genesis. "Joan of Arc upper plate, with a Nelson Eddy lower. And just a suggestion of Attila the Hun, perhaps, at the edges? For integrity?"

"Perfect!" cried the PM, clapping his hands. "Perfect! What can I offer you in return? Ask and it shall be given."

* * *

The Hon. Fenella Strume-Clavering spat wretchedly, watched her blood swirl away into the sewage system with lead upon her heart. It was her fourteenth extraction.

"Now you're Goreign Gecretary," she whimpered, "I guppoge you'll gig up gentitry?"

"Au contraire," said Genesis, wiping his wonderful hands on a scented towel, "I shall always be a dentist first, and a Foreign Secretary second." His fine eyes veiled nobly. "Once dentistry gets into a man's blood, once he feels the pulse of the drill in his fingers, the smell of floss in his nostrils, he has given up more than his life, madame. He has given up his soul!"

The Hon. Fenella groped beneath her bloodstained gown and flung out a hand to touch his.

"Gake me wig you!" she cried. "I lug you, Gark!"

He stepped back, hand to his brow.

"I cannot, madame! I fear that destiny has shaped me for other ends. As a statesman, nay, as a dentist, I may not allow the slightest taint to impeach my honour and the honour of my calling! Return to your husband! Return to your little ones!" He paused a moment, and glanced down at his distracted slave. "Besides, madame, have I not this very instant removed your last remaining natural tooth? How could you thus take your place beside me, the first dental Foreign Secretary the world has ever seen, and you with nought but a mouthful of gums?"

With an unearthly, fearful shriek, the Hon. Fenella Strume-Clavering cast off her gown and staggered from the chair that had borne her through so many long years of unrequited passion. The surgery doors swung shut, and her gummy moans faded on the Marylebone air.

But the Rt. Hon. Garth Genesis, B.D.S., heeded them not. Bathed in the roseate glow of an English evening, his handsome form stood silhouetted in the surgery window, gazing out upon the teeth and embassies that awaited him, somewhere beyond the setting sun.

This excerpt from 'All Except The Bastard' by Alan Coren (Robson Books Ltd.) was first published in Punch magazine.

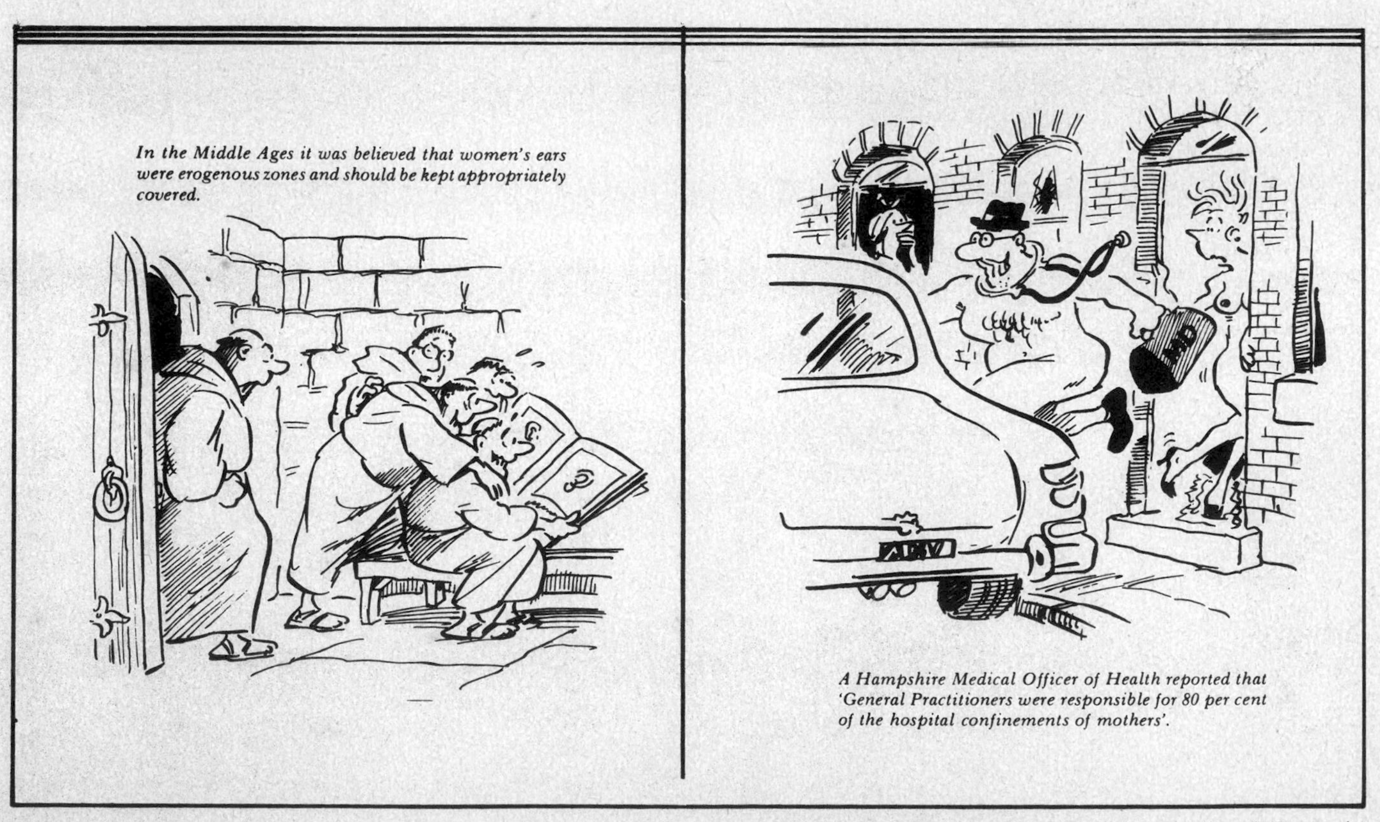

Cartoon's by Bill Tidy from 'Would You Believe It Doctor.'

And now, the least worst of...

The least worst of...

Hello Cheeky

TIM BROOKE TAYLOR, JOHN JUNKIN, BARRY CRYER

WAR —

We are proud to announce an exclusive. Prior to its publication by Pornopress, Frinton, we present extracts from the memoirs of the World War One hero and chicken molester, Lieutenant Colonel Retired.

Read to us by the author himself, in a posh voice.

We present: "All quiet on the Y fronts".

In 1914, as the war clouds were gathering over Europe, the war minister phoned me. I immediately packed my belongings in my old kitbag and smiled smiled smiled.

I hadn't got a lucifer to light my fag, so I smiled, boys, that's the style. I always say: "What's the use of worrying, it never is worthwhile . . . so . . . keep right on, to the end of the . . .

Scene moves to:

Aldershot Barracks . . . on a cold, grey morning . . . December 1914 . . . The NCO is interviewing our hero.

Right Sunny Jim . . . if you want to survive in this man's army . . . you gotta be hard, ruthless with a killer instinct.

Well, I'll try, bubbles.

Oh my gawd . . . still, you'll come in handy for regimental dances. The secret is . . . grasp the weapon firmly . . . grit your teeth, give a savage cry and plunge and withdraw like this . . . (CRY) . . . There . . . now you try.

Tim shouts like a dervish.

Right . . . it's easy to cope with army food, once you get the knack.

Things were pretty tough at Aldershot . . . or, so they tell me . . . I wasn't there. All too soon, our brave boys in brown . . .

It's not my colour.

Shut up, darling.

The war was hell . . . However, during those dark days, I was comforted by letters from Madge.

Dear Leroy . . . the upper lip's gone a bit soft . . . I think it's something they're putting in the water. I'm trying to pick up the threads of a normal life without you. I decided to take up golf once more. I got Carruthers to drive me out to the course and you'll be happy to hear I'm in the club again.

Scene moves to July 1916 . . . the Somme.

How are things, sergeant?

Not too good, sir, Living quarters are pretty cramped.

Really?

Yes . . . last week Higgins caught trench mouth and we billeted four of the lads in it. But you're an inspiration to us all sir. Standing there so tall and proud in all this mud. I don't know how you can do it, sir.

Bit of a cheat actually sergeant . . . I'm standing on my batman . . . however, I've got some good news for you. Gather round men . . . Scroggins, don't do that. I know you haven't seen your wife for two years, but that's no excuse . . . dancing with the cook . . . it's bad for morale.

Some time later came that unforgettable Christmas Day that has gone down in history . . .

A solo mouth organ plays "Silent Night."

Here, sarge . . . I couldn't believe my eyes . . .

Don't bother me now lad . . . Scroggins' wife is divorcing him and she's citing the cook.

No sarge . . . Nobby Thunderblast suddenly said it was the season of goodwill and peace and started to walk towards the German trenches.

What happened?

Believe it or not, the Germans came out of their trenches and started playing football with him.

That's wonderful.

Not really . . . they're using him as the ball.

Meanwhile, on a lily pad . . . two frogs are talking . . .

You're late.

Yes, got stuck in somebody's throat.

While we're here, let's have a game of leap-person.

Can't . . . gotta fly.

Where?

On the end of my tongue.

* * * *

I say, you chaps . . . I went to a take-away sauna last night.

What happened?

They set fire to my trousers and threw a bucket of water over me. Then they arranged for me to be beaten on the way home.

How do they do that?

They've got branches everywhere.

* * * *

Sing
Sing a song
Sing out loud
Sing out strong
Why?
There's no lock on the toilet.

* * * *

THE NEWS — Tim Brooke Taylor, John Junkin and Barry Cryer can be relied on to give you the important items.

Here is a Newsflash. Television viewers will be unable to see tonight's episode of Crossroads as Amy Turtle has rolled over on her back and can't get up. And with that, over to the sports desk . . .

Mount Anunda, in the Himalayas, is to be climbed by a team from the BBC Sports Sports Department. Eddie Waring said today . . .

It'll be the first time I've been up Anunda.

ON BBC 2 tonight's "Call My Bluff" has been cancelled as Jim Callaghan refused to appear in case somebody did.

At London Zoo today, head keeper, George Clenching, fought for an hour with a giant penguin that had escaped from its enclosure. It later turned out to be the head waiter from the Savoy in his lunchbreak. His wife said later: "This has upset him so I've put him to bed with a hot water bottle and a raw fish".

I studied yoghourt, you know.

Don't you mean . . .

No . . . I used to stand on my head in a bowl of sour milk and stuff raspberries up my nose.

I saw one of those mystics once. Held his breath for an hour and a half.

How did he do that?

I don't know . . . he died before he could tell us.

* * * *

Do you know I take four morning papers every day . . . does annoy the neighbours.

Why?

It's theirs I take.

I read the Mail myself but I get a Guardian for the wife.

Why?

If I don't, she's after that milkman like a whippet.

By the way, did you see my wife in the Mirror this morning?

No, just me.

No, there was a photograph of her opening a supermarket.

That's nice.

Not really . . . she was using a crowbar.

What on earth possessed her to do that?

She'd spent all the housekeeping money.

What on?

The crowbar.

* * * *

I think my M.P.'s coming round in favour of capital punishment.

What makes you say that?

He hanged his wife yesterday.

I was going to lobby my M.P. last week, but I don't know how you do it. I've heard he quite enjoys it, though.

Stop press. We have just heard that the head waiter, Ernesto Salvadori Lump, is suing Mr. Clenching for acute mental anguish and bending his dicky.

* * *

It's been reported that Max Bygraves has been going round the country, making speeches on behalf of Margaret Thatcher?

He's been saying: "I want to sell you a Tory".

With grateful thanks to the authors of the scripts and also to the kind help we received from the staff of the BBC Script Library.

signs off

SLOW
(CONCEALED ENTRANCES)
NO OVERTAKING FOR
THE NEXT 200 YRS

BEWARE
OF CROSS
TRAFFIC

HE v SHE

He versus She — the longest-running battle in the world. Talk about the Hundred Years War (the what?), we could all pack one of those into an ordinary working week any time. The trimmings may change, the small-arms fire get more sophisticated, BUT . . . it's been HER against HIM or, as I see it, HIM against HER (because naturally **I** *am all sweetness and logical light) since literally heaven only knows when. And quite right too. A good fight is always worth it for the peace that comes after.*

And I don't see things really changing that much — we may all have a touch of the Danny La Rues about us these days and marriage is supposed to be only for the birds (and a Burton or a Taylor now and again) — but the tug-of-war goes on. And long may it continue because, as we all know, when the snap goes out of the elastic, the whole thing falls down.

K.B.

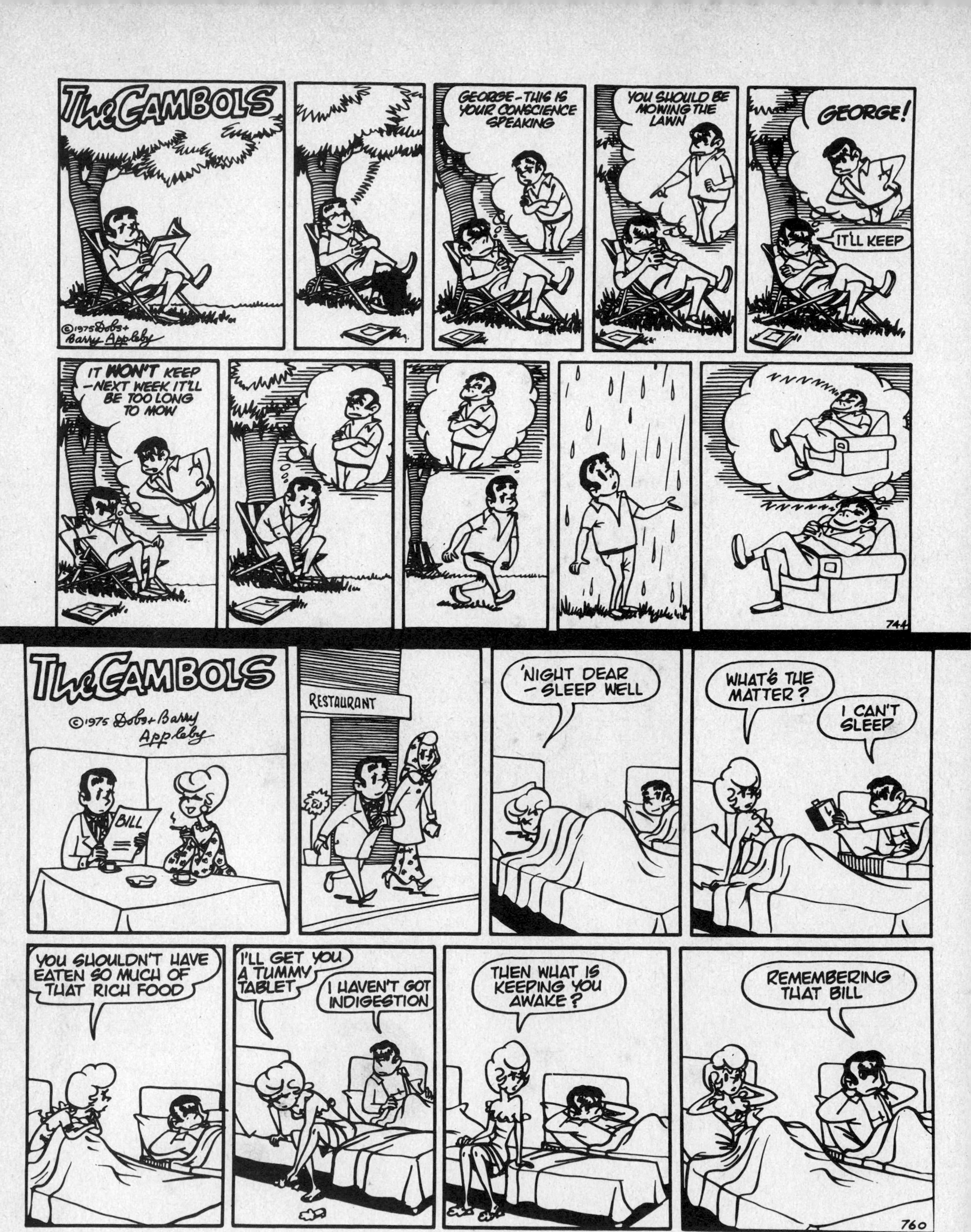

First published in The Sunday Express

AND SOME BASIC ADVICE ON AN IMAGINARY DOMESTIC PROBLEM

SHARING THE BEDROOM WITH A NEUROTIC WIFE

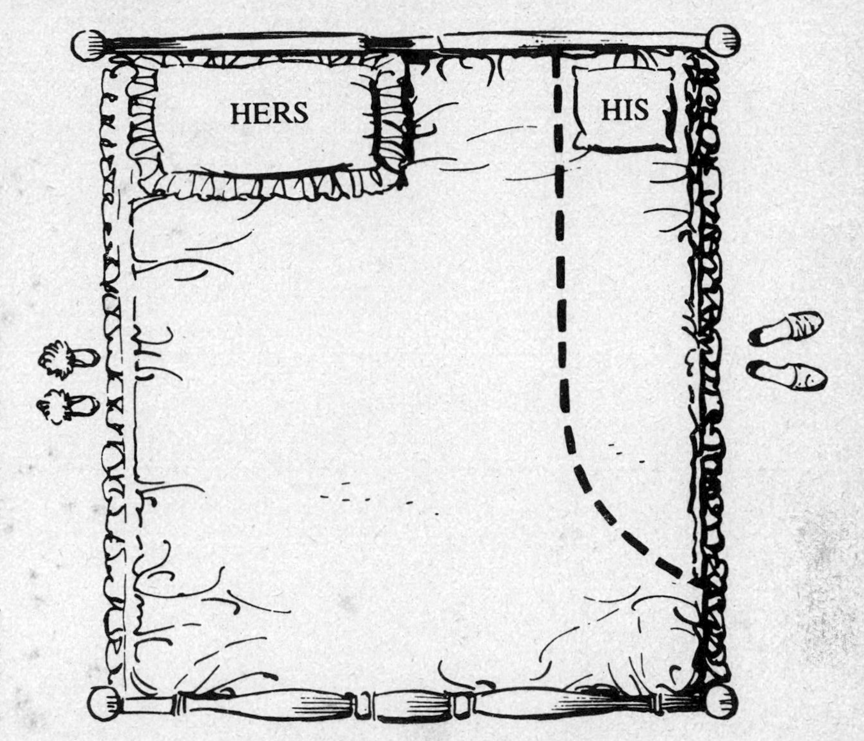

There are times when you must share the bedroom, or even your bed, with your wife. This of course brings up a multitude of problems.

The reason is that there is a fundamental difference of opinions between the sexes as to the intent of a bedroom. Husbands think of it as a place to display affections and promptly go to sleep afterwards. To a wife, a bedroom has other, more subtle meanings.

For her, a bedroom is an enclosure designed primarily for the purpose of talking things over. It has four walls and the acoustics make arguments sound more imposing. The husband is cornered at last. There is no way he can leave the premises without attracting her attention. And he just can't jump out of bed and take a walk around the block wearing only his pyjamas or less.

To make bedrooms even more practical for her use, there are beds in them. This piece of furniture represents a utilitarian item to a husband, but not to a wife. To her, a bed is at once a playground, an analyst's couch, a soap box, a camping ground, an athletic field, and a place to hold meetings with her as the Main Speaker.

Trying to get away from it all, many husbands spend their nights in twin beds. Others, in an attempt to get out of hearing distance altogether, establish residence in separate sleeping quarters. Neither of these solutions is completely satisfactory, however, for it makes love-making a complicated —and sometimes impossible— undertaking.

Less radical methods prove to be more workable. Hiding under the blanket or mattress offers temporary relief. Even more effective is use of the so-called Murphy bed which swings up against the wall at a mere pull of a lever. This type of bed, however, requires agility and quick reflexes. You must be able to roll out of it before it starts moving upwards lest you find yourself flattened against the wall in a vertical position — and still very much next to your spouse.

Sharing the same bed can become a source of controversy between the two interested parties. Both need room to sleep comfortably. As in all human relationships, your sense of fair play should be your guide. Use jurisdictional standards as they apply to property rights between husband and wife; i.e., ninety per cent of the estate goes to her, ten per cent to you.

Excerpt from 'How To Live With a Neurotic Wife' reproduced by permission of Frederick Muller Ltd.

by STEPHEN BAKER

B. C. Cartoons by Johny Hart © Fawcett Publications Inc. N.Y.

Every home should have one

THERE ARE aspects of women's lib that give me a nightmare in which all the men I have ever liked are being carted to the guillotine while I sit knitting in a ringside seat. Beside me is Germaine Greer, on the spot reporting for *Spare Rib,* while Jilly Cooper tries to work out a pun on "This Little Piggy," and Katherine Whitehorn gathers in-depth material for "Man," the first subject in her series on "Planned Obsolescence."

"Oughtn't they to have a trial?" shouts Mary Stott, so they bring on Jill Tweedie as counsel for the defence and Anna Coote as judge. All highly unlikely, of course. I can't knit and in such elevated company I would be too far at the back to see a thing. But it makes me think about starting a "Let's-be-friends-with-men" week.

Granted that for centuries female footstools were a male fashion. But honestly whose fault was it? If the first seven years of a child's life fathers the man, then the hand that rocked the cradle let the side down. A blank plastic mind to model and what did they do? Fashioned it just like Pappa's.

To start even further back, who told man he was superior unless it was a woman? From what I have read all that God did after the apple was show him the untamed wilderness and say, "Dig that, man," which should have left women with enough time on their hands to invent the wheel and be Dr. Schweitzer.

But now those bad old days are behind us and every woman has a right to her share of the ulcers. No longer need Fiona feel her sex has barred her from becoming a sewer-person; those kinky rubber thigh boots can be hers by law.

No union can complain if the woman gets the job as the rocket expert while her lover is left to look after the experimental mice—though he may if she takes the count-down into her private life. No need to wonder if anything he can do you can do better, just sign on for the deep drift and find out.

But as you buy your "I am a Woman" button to pin on your "Woman-Power" T-shirt remember somewhere in your "Liberated Woman's Appointments Book" to keep a date for Man.

Prone to illness, slow to recover, dead a good 10 years before us. Short on chromosomes, vulnerable to heart attacks, colour blindness, epilepsy and hysteria (remember that last time you were late?). He needs all the protection we conservationists can give him.

Now that woman is no longer the echo of man's ego why not let him try on some of our cast-off roles? Many a man may be yearning to be regarded as a sex object with a chance to end up as the plaything of some rich sugar mummy, instead of being wanted for his ability to clean out the top gutters, empty mouse-traps, move the wardrobe and hoist the ladder into place for you to clean the windows.

If women's magazines are anything to go by, he is also still faced with the choice of being strong, clever, rich, reliable, 6ft., witty and virile, or dropping dead.

Unless he is willing to change a tyre for a complete stranger who happens to be a woman. Then he can be short, stout, balding, bullet-headed and the most desirable man on earth. If it comes to keeping men around or taking lessons in car maintenance, what else can I say?

By Catherine Drinkwater

First published in the Western Mail.

SOME SOUND ADVICE ON COURTING

from RONNIE BARKER'S Book of Boudoir Beauties

A girl should never try to be too nonchalant (never lie on the floor just to show off your new shoes) . . .

. . . Or go out of her way to appear comic.

On the other hand, being ready to defend one's honour to this extent will probably frighten him off anyhow. (This is actually a photograph of a well-known landlady in Colwyn Bay, whose motto was "Stand by to repel all boarders".)

Pretending you had forgotten he was coming, and shouting "Come in, Mildred" at the sound of his knock can prove effective in dealing with the more bashful suitor.

But make sure it isn't the gas-man's day to call—otherwise he may spend twenty minutes checking your boiler.

Published by Hodder & Stoughton Ltd.

Ernie It doesn't matter.

Dame Flora It does matter, Mr Wise, it matters a lot to me and I won't have you upset like this – all right, I'll be delighted to appear in your play.

Ernie *(delighted)* You will!

Dame Flora I'll be honoured to speak your words, Mr Wise. *(Rise)* Now I must go. The car is outside.

Ernie *(takes Dame Flora's hand)* Looking forward to having you in my play, Dame Flora. We'll be in touch.

Dame Flora I look forward to that. Goodbye. *(Exits).*

Eric *(pulls her back)* It's raining like mad outside, you'll need this. *(Hands her stick of parasol. Dame Flora reacts then exits).*

Eric Happy now, Ern?

Ernie Gosh, I'll say! I'll be happier still when we get out of this house. Let's go now before the real owner gets back.

Chauffer enters.

Chauffeur Where do you want the luggage?

Dame Flora enters.

Dame Flora Just there. *(Chauffer exits)* Oh it's good to be home again.

Ernie *(quietly to Eric)* It's Dame Flora's house.

They both edge towards door.

Dame Flora Boys, please don't go, stay and have some of my drink. *(Takes bottle from Eric)* It's the 83.

Both 83?

Dame Flora 83 bottles for fifteen and nine.

Eric and Ernie give sickly smiles and slowly exit.

From 'The Best of Morecambe & Wise' by Eddie Braben published by The Woburn Press.

PETER USTINOV

As Quoted by DICK RICHARDS

The main weakness of the Liberals in Britain is that their platform is occupied by both other parties.

After Filming "Spartacus" Ustinov insisted that he would never again wear a toga or its equivalent:

To handle a toga properly you have to watch a woman very carefully and notice how she walks and sits down. This type of attention can be grievously misunderstood.

Some passing comments on America (which he loves) and the American way of life.

In America, through pressure of conformity, there is freedom of choice, but nothing to choose from.

America is going through a crisis within itself. It is something like Palestine must have been before Christ appeared, a country of minor prophets. Unfortunately, America is also highly concerned with major profits.

In America most people now have an annual check-up every month.

In the past seventy years man's capacity for displacing himself through space has increased to a far greater extent than it ever did from pre-history to 1900. All that has *not* improved perceptibly are man's actions when he arrives at the end of his journey.

Priest's – and politicians for that matter – should regard themselves as entertainers at least in so far that it's the entertainer's primary task to keep the audience awake.

One of Ustinov's favourites: A man visited Israel and asked to see the tomb of the Unknown Soldier. He was taken to a marble mausoleum near Tel Aviv and on it was carved: "Herman J. Ginsbergh (B. 1883 d. 1917)."

He said: "But I thought the soldier was supposed to be unknown?" The guide replied: "As a soldier he was unknown – but as a furrier –!"

From 'The Wit Of Peter Ustinov'

OFFDAYS

Be it never so humble, there's no place like somewhere else than home when you're sick and tired and want to get away from it all. Getting there is what hurts most. First and worst way has got to be the car, mainly because ten million other people will have chosen the same day, time, route and destination as you have. This causes something called traffic jams (though there's actually nothing sweet about them) which lead to frayed tempers, fractious children, yelling drivers, bent bumpers, and even divorce. This will not, however, stop us — and the other ten million—from going by car again next year.

The sky can look awfully sweet and empty in comparison — until you get up there, jammed in three abreast, six deep, eating your cardboard and plastic meals with your knees up to your chin, and worrying about hijackers — not to mention queueing for loos that are so small and triangular you have to go sideways, and some lout has pinched all the miniature soaps and emptied the free-blob hand lotion bottles before you can get your own sticky mitts on them.

*And when you finally get there—wherever there happens to be—the weather breaks (along with the local political situation), the food is awful, the rows start (oh those lovely lips-set, teeth-clenched, voice-down-***please** *holiday fights) and another vacation bites the dust. Which doesn't mean we won't all start saving up for next year right away.*

K.B.

After Dinner Mints III.

An English Archbishop making his first official visit to the U.S.A. was duly warned of the dangers of being misquoted by the tough press reporters of that country. So he was determined to guard his tongue and when upon arrival at New York Airport he was presented to the throng of reporters in the V.I.P. room, he braced himself for the first question. This came from a tough Brooklyn-speaking reporter, who asked if the Archbishop intended to visit any of the famous New York Clubs with their strip tease dancers.

The Archbishop thought carefully for a moment and replied with a little smile, "Are there any such Clubs in New York?"

Everyone laughed and applauded, and he was still congratulating himself upon his clever reply the next morning when the first daily newspapers were delivered. There, staring from the headlines was the bold caption –

Limey Bishop's First Question – "Are there any strip tease clubs in New York?"

One of the best known examples of compromise took place in a little Scottish borough. The Provost, visiting the city chambers, passed the Town Clerk's room, and looking through the window saw the typist sitting on his knee. For a little Scottish borough that was not good enough, and the Provost called a meeting of the Town Council to decide what to do. A suggestion was made that they should get rid of the Town Clerk. But he was a good Town Clerk and they are difficult to come by. Then the suggestion was made they should sack the typist. But she was a good typist and they are even more difficult to find and keep than a good Town Clerk. It seemed they were in a real predicament until a little man in the corner offered the suggestion which was acted upon—and that was that they should buy a blind for the window.

A famous personality was presenting prizes at a girls' school, and tried to say something more original than the usual "congratulations", "well done" etc. to each prize winner. The girls came up in age groups and eventually the Head Girl stepped on to the platform to collect several prizes she had won. She was a good-looking girl of about 17 and the famous man thought that as this was her last term it would be appropriate to ask her "And what are you going to do when you leave school?" The girl looked at him very coyly and said "Well I *had* thought of going straight home."

A university professor was addressing an early morning lecture.

"I've found that the best way to start the day is to exercise for five minutes, take a deep breath of air and then finish with a cold shower. Then I feel rosy all over."

A sleepy voice from the back of the room:

"Tell us more about Rosy."

THE LAST WORD

A speaker at a dinner went on and on and on. A diner told the chairman: "Hit him on the head with your mallet". The chairman struck out but by a mistake hit the guest of honour. The guest of honour started to slowly disappear under the table semi-conscious and was then heard to mutter: "Hit me again, I can still hear him".

more from de Emerald Oil

A Irishman went to London and found himself in the Underground late one night. Seeing a notice DOGS MUST BE CARRIED ON THE ESCALATOR, he moaned to himself, 'Where am I going to find a dog at this hour of the night?'

Have you heard about the Irishman who got a pair of water skis for Christmas?
He's still going around looking for a lake with a slope.

One day the phone rang and when the Irishman answered he hung up immediately.
'Who was that?' asked his boss.
'Some fool saying it was a long distance from New York. I told him everybody knew that.'

Two Irishmen were out shooting duck. The first Irishman took aim, fired, and shot down a duck which landed at his feet.
'You could have saved the shot', said the second Irishman, 'the fall would have killed it anyway.'

A Irishman joined the army, but forgot to take his overcoat with him. His mother posted the coat to him, with the following note:

Dear Son,
I'm sending on your overcoat which you forgot. To save postage I've cut off the buttons.
Your loving Mother.
P.S. You'll find the buttons in the pocket.

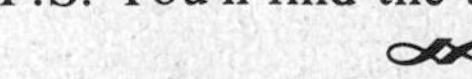

What do you find at the top of a Irish ladder?
A STOP sign.

'Hello, is that Tralee two, double two, double two?'
'No, you've got the wrong number. This is Tralee double two, double two, two'.
'Sorry for troubling you in the middle of the night'.
'That's all right, I had to get up anyway because the phone was ringing'.

As the Titanic was sinking, a Irishman was swimming madly round the ship, shouting 'Where's the dance, where's the dance?'
'What do you mean, "dance"?' asked a drowning passenger.
'I heard an announcement only ten minutes ago', said the Irishman, 'a-band-on ship, a-band-on ship'.

A Irishman bought a large engagement ring for his girlfriend.
'Ooh', she gasped, 'is it a real diamond?'
'If it's not', said the Irishman, 'I've just been done out of £1.50'.

A Irishman went to the doctor and complained that every time he drank a cup of tea he got a sharp pain in his eye.
'Have you tried taking the spoon out of the cup?' asked the doctor.

A Irishman vistited his psychiatrist and said, 'Look Doc, I've got two questions to ask you'.
'Right', said the psychiatrist, 'ask me the first question'. 'Doc', said the Irishman, 'could I possibly be in love with an elephant'.
'Of course not', said the psychiatrist, 'what's your other question?'
'Do you know of anybody who wants to buy a very large engagement ring?'

A Irishman was on the boat to Holyhead when there was a shout of 'Man overboard'. The Captain shouted 'throw in a buoy', so the Irishman grabbed a little eight-year-old boy and threw him into the water.
'No, you fool', said the Captain, 'I meant a cork buoy'.
'How the heck was I to know what part of Ireland he was from?' roared the Irishman.

A fellow wanted to have his house renovated, but thought that all the estimates he received were too high. Finally he consulted a Irish building contractor who came to view his house.
'I'll completely redecorate your bedroom for £15', said the Irishman.
'Great', said the fellow, 'all the others wanted at least £100'. At this the Irishman rushed over to the window and shouted out 'Green side up, green side up'.
'How about the bathroom?' asked the fellow, 'the others wanted at least £250'.
'My men and I will do it for £38.57', said the Irishman, whereupon he rushed to the window and shouted 'Green side up, green side up'.
'Well you seem to be the man I've been looking for', said the fellow, 'just tell me one thing, why do you go to the window and shout "Green side up, green side up?"
'That's just technical information to my workmen', said the Irishman, 'they're laying a lawn next door'.

Oh I do like to be......

A small boy dropped some ice-cream over the edge of the pier. It landed on the bare chest of a man who was sunbathing on the beach below.
Wiping it off with his towel, he mutters, "that seagull must live in a refrigerator.'

Keith: 'That girl who won the beauty contest doesn't seem very intelligent.'
Roger: 'No, she ignored me as well.'

"What on earth do you want your knitting for?"

The Englishman on holiday on the Isle of Wight soon got bored with the rich Texan who was staying at the same hotel, and was always boasting about how much bigger and better everything was 'back in the States'.
Pondering how he could 'best' him while they strolled together along the seafront, the Englishman saw the QE2 a few hundred yards from the shore. Quick as a flash, he leaned over the railings and shouted, 'Come in Number Seven. Your time's up!'

Their seaside romance was growing into love.
'You are a girl in a thousand,' he whispered to her as they strolled along the pier one evening.
The girl burst into tears and said, 'Have there been that many others?'

'I'm forgetting men tonight,' said Rita as she and her friend swayed into the seafront coffee-bar.
'So am I,' said the friend. 'I'm for getting two of them as soon as we can.'

A little boy was crying on the beach, 'I can't find my mummy. I'm lost.'
As he walked along the beach in this way, holiday-makers gave him pennies and sweets to console him.
After about twenty minutes, somebody said, 'But I know where your mummy is, little boy.'
'So do I,' he hissed. 'Shut up and go away.'

Two seagulls swooped over the beach on a really hot Bank Holiday. There wasn't a spare inch of sand to be seen. One seagull turned to the other and said sadly, 'It takes all the skill out of it, doesn't?'

"Let it down or carry it yourself."

It was a really old-fashioned seaside boarding-house, complete with aspidistra and antiques. A stag's head graced the wall in the lounge.
'Now,' said a boarder, looking at it. 'That deer must've been going a tremdous speed when it hit the other side of that wall.'

Rita: 'You remind me of the sea.'
John: You mean—wild, romantic and restless?'
Rita: 'No. You make me sick.'

'How about a kiss?' the young man asked as he walked home with a girl he had only just met at the dance.
'I have scruples,' she replied rather primly.
'That's OK.,' he assured her. 'I've been vaccinated.'

PETER SIMPLE REPOR

Railway

RAILWAY enthusiasts a
alike will be interested in th
plans for the famous stat
Hoke (Staffs) which, as I
day, has won the Briggs M
dirtiest station in Britain
running.

In a far-reaching reorga
Lampton is to lose its oth
(Bog Lane End), on the old
This station, though not
Lampton-on-Hoke, is equal
and is said to be haunted by
refreshment-room manager
(1872-1908).

All facilities will now
Lampton-on-Hoke, a notab
litter conservationists, who l
demolish the station tooth
volunteered to put in a few h
the station even dirtier than
possible. They hope to get a
Council, which is interested i
potential as the Dirtiest Ra
World.

Mr. Jim Grudge, brother o
Stretchford North, now Su
Nerdley, is to take charge of
of the unmanned halts
Newcastle-on-Stretch, whic
sidence are now almost enti

Mr. Don Nobes, the prese
Lampton (Bog Lane End) is
service and has been offer
"Friends of Litter" organisa
Officer. Particularly fine ite
the station (such as the famo
Fungi from the old waiting r
be added to the Lampton-o
The rest will be put up for
Nerdley Town Hall in the ne

From 'The World of Peter Simple' published by The Daily Telegraph

'Your advertisement said that your hotel was only minutes from the sea,' protested the holidaymaker. 'It took me nearly half an hour to get there this morning.'

'Ah,' explained the manager, 'you've been walking. We don't cater for pedestrians.'

Two men were fishing from the end of the pier when one of them landed a mermaid. He had a good look at her, and then threw her back in the sea.

'Why? ' asked his friend.

'How? ' said the other.

A coach party of women was being shown a spot on the west coast of Scotland where a waterfall fell three hundred feet into the sea.

'This, ladies,' said the coach driver, 'is a natural waterfall. Thousands of gallons of water fall into the sea every second. And if you'll just stop talking for a moment you'll be able to hear the deafening roar of the waters.'

It was the last day of their holidays. Tomorrow, the young couple would go their different ways and their seaside friendship would end.

'I'd like to do something different tonight,' said the girl.

'OK.,' agreed the lad. 'You try to kiss me, and I'll slap your face.'

AWAY

Foreign

With

"Paris! Paree! What
Napoleon, the Revoluti
the Queen of cities calls
class non-return tourist
undesirable coloured a

At the airport there v
fastened my safety belt,
and read The Times. One
belt, swallowed by boil

Arriving at the Hotel,
had been built in 1803 –
crack of noon shouting
breakfast of porridge a

I next joined a crowd
At midday we were led t
tourists:

The lady next to me h
Just so they didn't think I
a coloured pencil and a
Kong."

Book C
Card P
Church
Confect
Dairy F
Divers
Drinker
Footbal
Introve
Knitters

MAINLY FOR MOTORISTS...

Definitions

Motorist—One who keeps pedestrians in good running condition.

Pedestrian—A man who has found a place to park his car.

Split second—The time between the lights changing and the fellow behind sounding his horn.

Question: When does the pedestrian have the right of way?

Answer: After he's placed in the ambulance.

Garage Hint: To ensure safe motoring, see that every nut is tight, except the one at the wheel.

"Oh for heaven's sake – take him through again."

Some Observations—for speed-limit breakers

It is the overtakers who make work for the undertakers.

It is better to be a few minutes late than arrive dead on time.

It is better to be behind time in this world than to arrive before your time in the next.

Use care, the best motoring spirit.

A pedestrian is often prone to be careless, and if he is careless he is often prone.

A careful driver is one who has just spotted a police patrol.

When you've passed your driving test, it does not mean that you are entitled to pass everything else.

"That's only an estimate of course, it will cost more than that."

The Lorrydriver stopped to pick up a female hitch-hiker and immediately got into conversation. The lady claimed to be a witch and of course the driver did not believe her. Then she put her hand on his knee and he turned into a lay-by.

When stopping a motorist, the constable said, "Do you realise one of your rear lights isn't working". The motorist got out of his car walked to the back, kicked the bumper and the light came on. "Very good" said the constable. "Now kick your windscreen in and see if your tax comes up to date."

BUN FLIGHT

by BARRY NORMAN

First Printed in The Guardian 6. 4. 77

JUST AFTER take-off the stewardess came round wearing the flash-on/flash-off smile that is issued, along with the uniform, to all Americans who have any dealings with the public and distributing little brochures in which were listed the delights on offer in what the airline called its "Gold Plate Service."

And, as I read, one line sprang out as it were from the printed page, filling me with a strange excitement. "An ever-changing array of tarts," it proclaimed and the prospect of the next ten hours or so seemed suddenly brighter.

It was an American airline, naturally. Only an American airline would have the panache, the showmanship, the sheer chutzpah to turn its jumbo jets into so many flying bordellos, knowing that what the tired businessman and the knackered journalist need as they wing their way across the Atlantic is not some rotten old in-flight movie but an ever-changing array of tarts offering Gold Plate Service.

And what tarts they appeared to be—tarts with thrilling names like Rocky Road (a big smouldering girl, no doubt, in leather knickers) and California Orange (a Los Angeles redhead, perhaps, who hadn't quite made it in the movies and had turned instead to the honourable profession of airborne tart). I was musing on this, quietly anticipating the pleasures to come, when the stewardess threw a glass of wine and a cup of coffee in my lap. Well, she didn't actually throw them. She just dropped a load of cutlery on to my tray, causing the wine and coffee to spread darkly across my coat and trousers.

I uttered a couple of deletable expletives and she got a dry cloth and knelt beside me in the aisle, dabbing amiably at my nether regions, and another stewardess came by and said: "You wanna pay for that wine now?" Flash on-flash off.

"No I bloody well don't," I said and those who know me well might have detected a faint note of testiness in my voice. "Your mate's just thrown it all over me."

The first stewardess finished her ministrations and stood up. "I didn't do that on purpose, you know," she said somewhat huffily. An odd choice of words, it seemed to me—even an ominous choice of words when the other one came back and said the same thing. "She didn't do that on purpose, you know."

The clear implication there, as I see it, is that while on this occasion the hurling of a glass of wine and a cup of coffee into a passenger's lap was simply an unfortunate accident such as could happen to anyone, they could both imagine — or even remember — occasions on which the hurling of a glass of wine and a cup of coffee into a passenger's lap was a deliberate act, done with malice aforethought.

Of course, it could be that what we had was a problem of semantics, two nationalities separated by a different use of the same language.

(A few days earlier on another American flight a voice on the intercom had said: "Good morning, ladies and gen'lemen, this is your captain. We'll be in the air momentarily . . ." and I'd clutched in panic at a passing stewardess and said, "Look, for God's sake tell him— momentarily isn't enough. I want to be in the air till we reach our destination." She'd given me a strange look and ignored me for the rest of the flight.).

But if it wasn't semantics I can only suppose that passengers who have wine and coffee thrown over them deliberately are the trouble-makers — people who, for some trifling medical reason, can't eat any of the dishes on the menu or complain that they've already seen the movie or insist on pressing the button for service. Or else people who cause unnecessary fuss by having wine and coffee spilt in their laps.

Air travel in these days of overcrowded jets is not for the individual. The individual is a nuisance. Air travel is for those who keep a low profile, never ask questions, bother the stewardesses as little as possible, and generally behave as though they've had a frontal lobotomy to render them docile.

As for that ever-changing array of tarts, well, that was a semantic rip-off if you like. What is a tart to an American is just another sticky bun to an Englishman.

Vive La FRANCE

The trouble with the French, of course, is that unless you speak the lingo, it's impossible to know whether or not they're being funny (and it's distinctly unfunny when they laugh garlic all over you). So here are a few wild Gallic inventions instead.

E 9 Spooncomber
For retrieving hairs that have inadvertantly fallen in the soup.

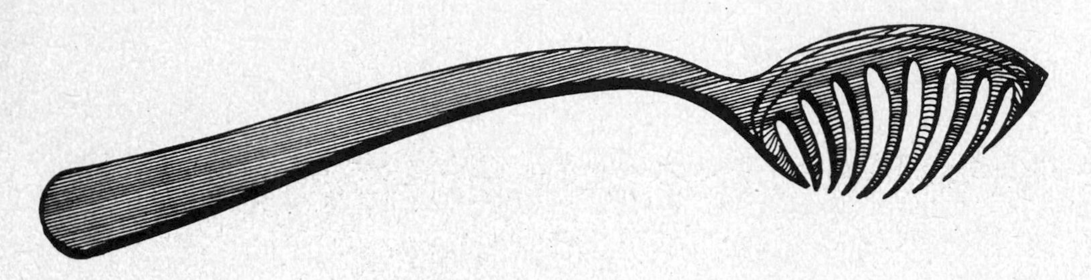

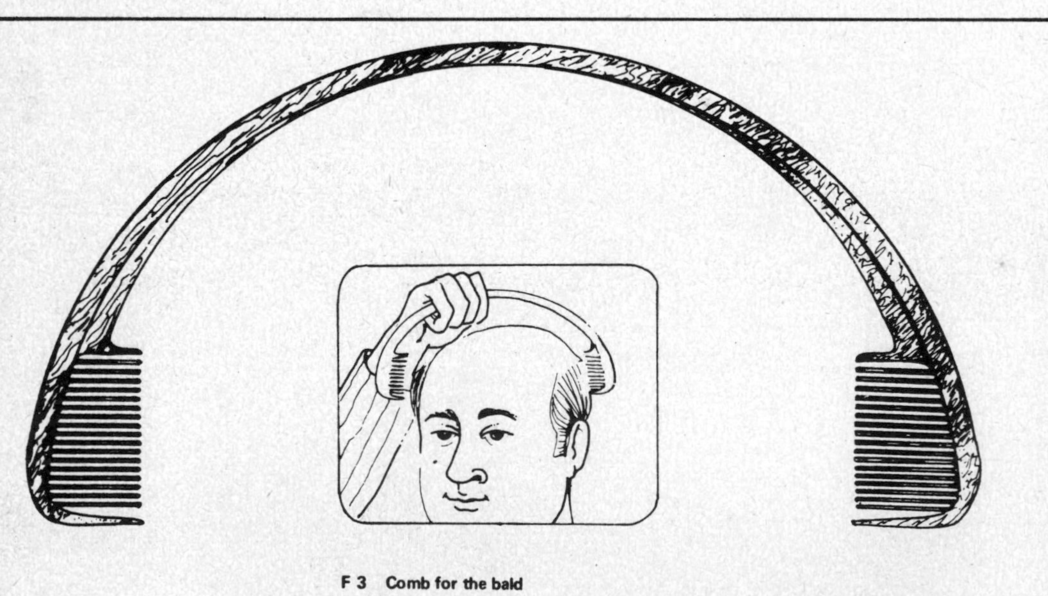

F 3 Comb for the bald

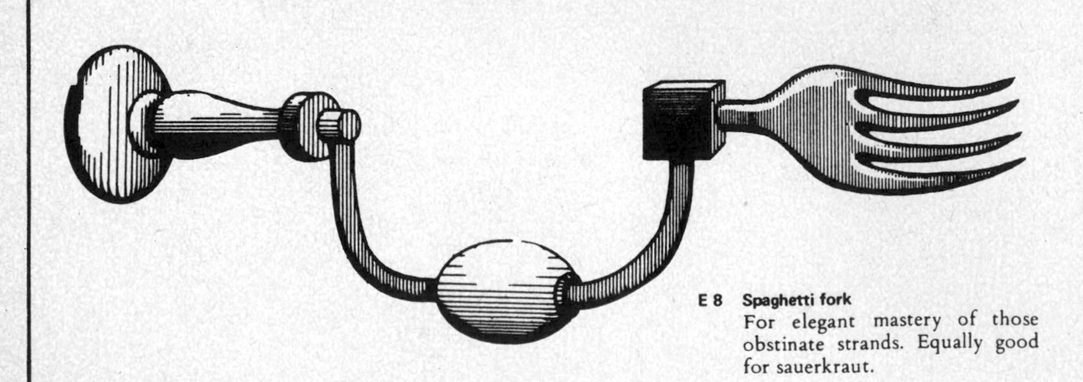

E 8 Spaghetti fork
For elegant mastery of those obstinate strands. Equally good for sauerkraut.

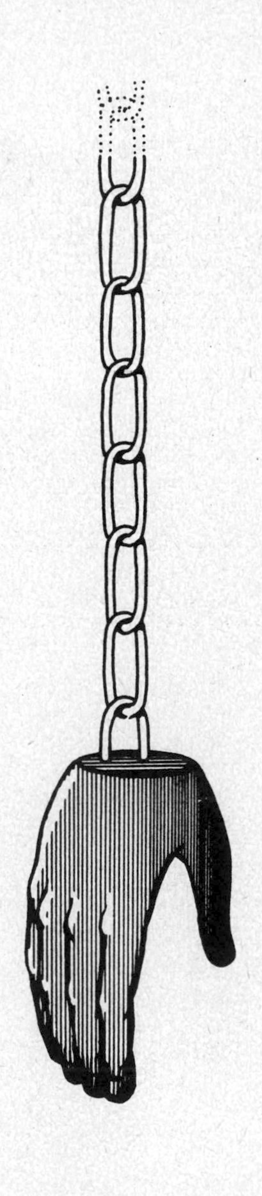

F 14 Novelty lavatory-chain handle
Hospitable and reassuring.

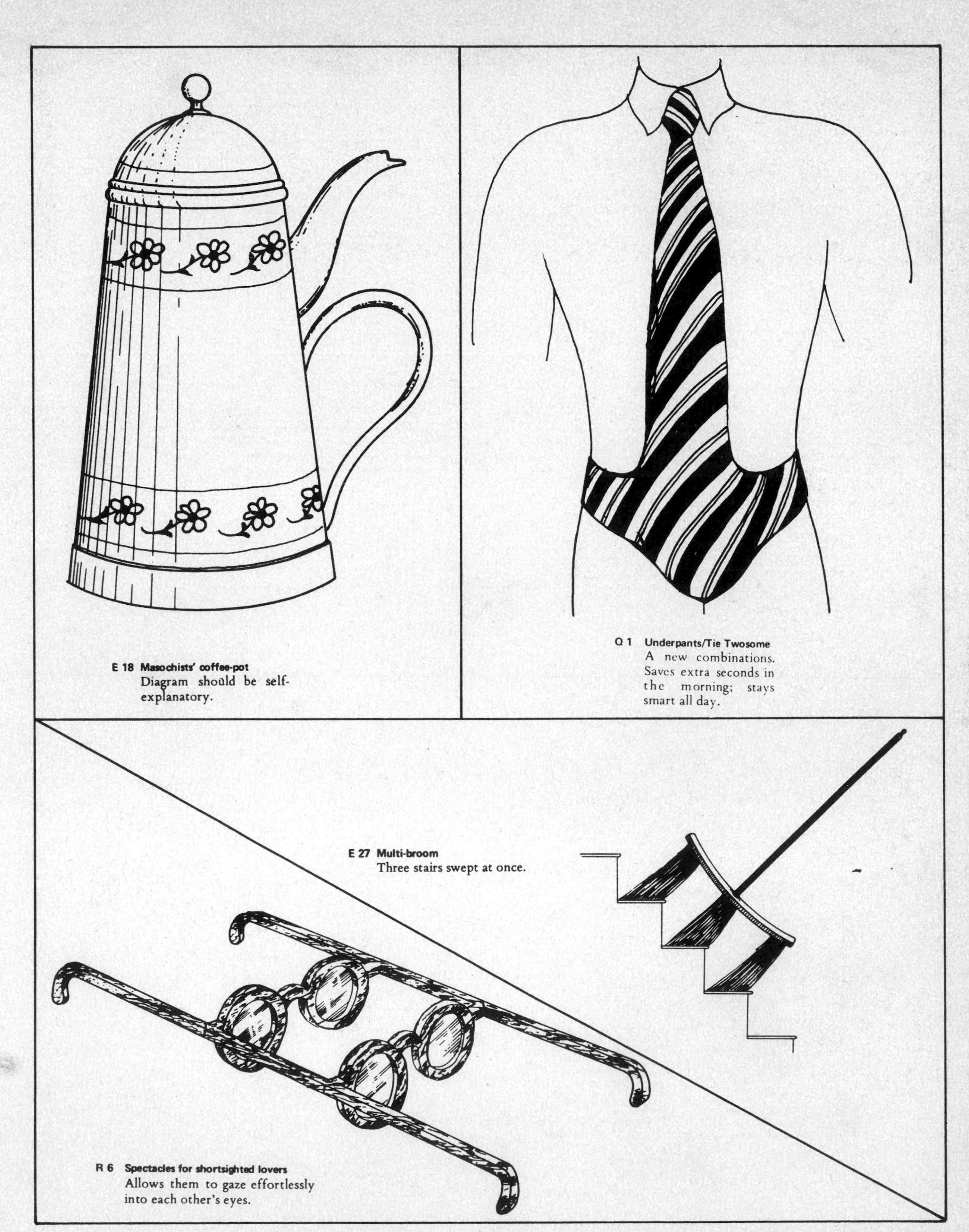

Pictures from 'Catalogue of Extraordinary Objects' by Jacques Carelman published by Abelard-Schuman Ltd.

Fare Dinkum

Don't imagine we can go jetting out to Australia and get around with our own lah-di-dah English. You'd better believe you'd have to take a short language course in Strine *before you take the trip. And this is how it goes:*

Let Talk Strine

or Austrylian as she is spoke.

AORTA:is the personification of the benevolently paternal welfare State to which all Strines — being firecely independent and individualistic — appeal for help and comfort in moments of frustration and anguish. The following are typical examples of such appeals. They reveal the innate reasonableness and sense of justice which all Strines possess to such a marked degree:

'Aorta build another arber bridge. An aorta stop half of these cars from cummer ninner the city — so a feller can get twirkon time.'

'Aorta mica laura genst all these prairlers and sleshers an pervs. Aorta puttem in jile an shootem.'

'Aorta stop all these transistors from cummer ninner the country. Look what they're doone to the weather. All this rine! Doan tell me it's not all these transistors — an all these hydrigen bombs too. Aorta stoppem!'

'Aorta have more buses. An aorta mikem smaller so they don't tike up half the road. An aorta put more seats innem so you doan tefter stann all the time. An aorta have more room innem — you carn tardly move innem air so crairded. Aorta do something about it.'

ENEMY: The limit of. As in: Enemy tether. Not to be confused with Emeny of the phrase 'Emeny jiwant?'

FLESH IN THE PEN: Momentary brilliance. As in: 'Ar, stoo gooder last, Sairndra, it's jessa flesh in the pen.' The derivation of this curious phrase is obscure. General etymological opinion is that it has come down from the time when the early Strine settlers fashioned pens from goose quills — often without first removing the goose. The phrase is believed originally to have been, 'gooseflesh in the pen', meaning shaky or illegible writing (caused by the struggles of the goose).

FURRY TILES: Sick humour for kiddies. These are stories which begin with the words, 'One spawner time . . .' and then describe in graphic and revolting detail various acts of murder, mayhem and treachery, such as '. . . he drew out a sharp knife and cut off the head of the wicked brother', and 'At nightfall they came to the edge of a deep forest and the young maiden then did what the witch had told her — she cut out the young huntsman's heart and threw it down the well. Then she wept bitter tears and could not be comforted and they lived happily ever after.'

Because of their violence and gloomy horror such stories are, naturally, very popular with young children, and it is surprising that so few Strine furry tiles exist. Those that do are usually variations on the theme of 'If we are returned to power . . .' or 'You may rest assured that I shall leave no stone unturned.'

GISSA: 'Please give me . . .' As in: 'Gissa lookcha alchbra.' This word is the subject of a curious sexual taboo; it may be used only by males. The female equivalent is Gimme, or Gimmier. As in: Gimmier nairm semmitchenna cuppa tea.'

GONNIE: Do you have any? As in: 'Gonnie epples?' 'Gonnie forby three oregon?' 'Gonnie newsa Bev?'

HEMBAIRG: A bag, carried by all Strine women, for the transport of personal possessions such as money, cigarettes, lipstick and a hairnkie.

LAIDAN: A short rest after the midday meal; a siesta.

LAZE AND GEM: Usual beginning of a public speech. Often combined with Miss Gem. As in: 'Miss gem, laze and gem. It gives me grape leisure . . .'

LONDGER RAY: Women's underclothing.

HEADER, MARY: Daughter of one of the early Strine graziers. She was responsible, after years of bitter struggle with the authorities, for the introduction of compulsory education for sheep. She thus lit a lamp which has continued to burn steadily down the years and many of today's famous Strine sheep must be grateful to her memory. One of her little lambs, Charles, who had followed her to school each day, eventually became an essayist and poet of considerable skill and composed the following song in memory of his sponsor:

> Mary Header little lamb:
> An intellectual nit.
> It never passed its first exam
> Because it couldn't sit.
>
> So Mary Header little lamb
> With vedgies and mint sauce.
> 'Oh, dearest lamb,' she cried, 'I am
> As hungry as a horse.'

MONEY: The day following Sunny. (Sunny, Money, Chewsdy, Wensdy, Thursdy, Fridy, Sairdy.)

RISE UP LIDES: Sharpened steel wafers, now usually stineless, used for shiving.

SCETTIN LAIRDER: It is becoming louder.

SCONA: A meteorological term. As in: Scona rine; scona clear up; scona be a grade A; etc.

SEMMITCH: Two slices of bread with a filling in between, e.g. M-semmitch; semmon semmitch; chee semmitch. When ordering semmitches the following responses are indicated:

A: Sell semmitches?
B: Air, emeny jiwant?
A: Gimmie utter martyr and an airman pickle. Emma chisit? (or Emma charthay?)
B: Toon nimepen slidy. (or Threen form smite).
B: Toon nimepen slidy. (or Threen form smite. A man is always expected to pay more for food than a woman is.)

SEX: Large cloth bags used as containers for such things as potatoes, cement, etc. As: Sex of manure, corn sex, etc. Also known as heshing bairgs.

SLY DROOL: An istrument used by engineers for discovering Kew brutes and for making other calculations.

STEWNCE: Persons engaged in learning something from books, or attending an educational institution, especially of the higher class; scholars; persons dedicated to the pursuit of knowledge. As in: Four stewnce were arrested and charged with offensive behaviour. Or: Plea sledge stewnce threw Exeter bystanner.

TAN CANCEL: The elected local government authority.

TO GORF: To leave suddenly; to begin flying. As in: 'He to gorf like a rocket'; 'He togorf like a batter to hell'. Antonym: To lairned. As in: 'He to gorf at tempest four, Annie lairnded a Tairsenden atterbat hapas nine.'

UPPENDAN: To and fro; backwards and forwards. As in: 'She walked uppendan Flinner Street farairs, and then she finey got a cabbome to Cannerby.'

X: The twenty-fourth letter of the Strine alphabet; also plural of egg; also a tool for chopping wood.

YEGGOWAN: Do you intend travelling to? As in: 'Yeggowan Rare Wick Sairdy?' or 'Yeggowan E. Smelpen on Wensdy? Ora yeggowan togota Sunkilta?'

ZARF TRAWL: Because after all. As in: 'Zarf trawl Leica nony doomy Bess.' or: 'Zarf trawl wee rony flesh and blood wennit Saul boiled down.'

Excerpt from 'Let Stalk Strine by Afferbeck Lauder published by Ure Smith Pty. Ltd.

"HERE COMES THE FLYING DOCTOR."

DOWNING IT DOWNUNDER

A local chucker-out

An old-time publican got sick and tired of the rowdies who brawled in his bar and did much damage to his property. Being no great fighter himself, he approached a local bruiser (who happened to be as Irish as Paddy's potatoes) and asked him to be the pub's official 'bouncer'.

Mick and the publican shook hands on the deal, which provided for a dollar to be paid to Mick every time he threw out a trouble maker.

Mick did his job well. He enjoyed every minute of it. Things went along in fine style until one evening, while Mick was having his tea, the publican rushed over to his place and shouted, 'Come quick! Danny Murphy's on the rampage! I'll give you *two* dollars to toss him out before he wrecks the joint!"

At these words Mick was aggrieved. He caught the publican by the lapels of his coat, with his great ham-like fists, and shook him till his teeth rattled.

'Arrh,' says Mick, 'it's a shocking thing whin you'll be comin' into me own home and offerin' me double money to bounce Danny Murphy—him that's me best friend. And I'll not be having it said I took money to bounce me ould mate. *But I'll do it for nothing.*'

Drinking water keeps you from getting stiff in the joints — if the joints will serve water. Like the tale of Paddy, the non-conformist Irish-Aussie who walked into the bar of a country pub and asked for a glass of water. And another. And another.

The publican charged him forty cents.

'Faith, that's a bit over the fince, isn't it?' Paddy growled.

'Hell!' says Mine Host indignantly. 'You come in here, sit down for an hour, sip six glasses of water through a straw— and expect all this for *nothing!* And now you'll rise from the chair, put on your hat, and calmly walk out . . .'

'And what do you expect me to do?' roared Paddy. 'Put me hat on and *stagger* out?

Tall & Shaggy–Aussie Style

The Great Australian Larrikin

as told by Billy Borker
in the Albion Hotel, Parramatta.

WHAT would be the best Australian story you ever heard, Billy?

The Great Australian Larrikin, as my father called it, is one of the best, I'd reckon, Jerome.

Have another drink and tell me about him.

Don't mind if I do. This fella's name was Dooley Franks. A real knockabout man. Lived here in Parramatta. Ran a double, did a bit of urging at the races, sold smuggled transistors. One night he went to Tommo's two-up school and won five hundred quid backing the tail. So he decided to join the Tattersall's Club. Up he choofs to the uniformed flunkey at the club door, wearing a polo neck jumper, suede shoes, and one of them small brimmed hats with a yellow feather in it. "Here, fill in this form," the flunkey says dubiously; "the committee will consider your application and let you know in due course." When the committee meets the secretary says: "This Dooley Franks is an urger. We can't have him in the club." The committee members could not have agreed more: most of them *used* to be urgers, see. "Dooley Franks hasn't got two pennies to clink together. Just tell him the joining fee—a hundred pounds—and that'll be the end of it." So they write Dooley a letter and he bounces back and slams a bundle of tenners on the counter in front of the flunkey. Well, the committee got really worried. The secretary says: "Tell him he has to have three sponsors, famous people, not Australians. The furthest he's ever been from Parramatta is to the Kembla Grange racecourse." They think they've got old Dooley Franks beat, see. So the flunkey tells him: "Three famous people not Australians." "Why didn't you say so in the first place?" Dooley says, "would have saved time and trouble. Eisenhower (he was President at that time), Khrushchev and the Pope. Just tell 'em Dooley Franks from Parramatta wants a reference."

He was joking, of course?

Wait till I tell yer. Don't spoil the story, mate, one of the best Australian stories ever told. Well, the committee got a shock, needless to say. Now, the secretary was a hard case, so he says: "Listen, this here Dooley Franks couldn't know Eisenhower, Khruschchev or the Pope. Tell you what we'll do. We'll offer to take him over to Washington, Moscow and Rome, in person. Then we'll hear no more about it." They write to Dooley Franks and he says: "All right with me. Air letters would be cheaper, but if you insist." The secretary says: "We're stuck with it now. We'll put in a hundred quid each and I'll go with him. It'll be the joke of the century." Away they go by air to Washington, up the steps to the White House. They wait around in corridors for about three days and eventually they get an appointment with one of Eisenhower's side-kicks. "I'm from Tattersall's Club, Sydney," the secretary says. The Yank is puzzled. "Sydney," he asks, "where's that?" "Australia," the secretary tells him. "Ah, yeah," the Yank replies. "That's where we sell all our old films to the television stations." "We want to see President Eisenhower," the secretary says. "You can't just come here and see the President. You have to have an appointment." Well, Dooley Franks is getting a bit impatient, see, so he says: "Listen, just tell Ike Dooley Franks wants to see him. The bloke who pinched six tins of petrol for him when his car ran out on the road to Paris. Dooley Franks from Parramatta." Well, the Yank goes away and comes back. "Mister Franks," he says, "why didn't you say so in the first place? President Eisenhower will see you right away." "Can I come too?" the secretary says. "No, the President wants to have a private chat with Mister Franks."

Surely he didn't actually know Eisenhower?

Well, he came back six hours later high as a kite. "Sorry to keep you waiting," he tells the secretary. "Me and Ike got talking old times over a few drinks and lost track of time." So they head off for Moscow.

Ah, don't tell me . . .

Up to the Kremlin gates with an interpreter they go. Freezing cold night, thirty-eight below. The secretary put over a spiel about the Tattersall's Club and Dooley tells the bloke on the gate: "Just tell Nikita that Dooley Franks from Parramatta wants to see him. Was treasurer of the Sheepskins For Russia appeal during the war, sailed on the North Sea convoys and sold Russian magazines on the Sydney waterfront." Well, to make a long story short, the same thing happens: Khrushchev wants to see Comrade Franks, and the secretary of the Tattersall's Club is left freezing in the Red Square. Dooley comes out eventually, and next day they head for Rome. And the secretary is thinking: What will I tell the committee when I get back? They'll never believe me. If he gets in to see the Pope, I'm going with him.

And did he?

Well, they see a cardinal, but he says you have to make an appointment for an audience with the Pope. So Dooley tells him: "Just say Dooley Franks from Parramatta; was an altar boy at St Patrick's Cathedral, got a brother a priest and a sister a nun." The cardinal comes back—if you don't believe me you can ask old Dooley himself—he says the Pope will grant a private audience to Mister Franks. The secretary begs to be let in. "I must see them together," he says. "His Holiness wishes to see only Mister Franks. But if you want to see them together you can stand down in the square. His Holiness will appear on the balcony at one o'clock and I'll arrange for Mister Franks to stand with him." Well, the secretary is desperate: what's he going to tell the committee? He goes away and comes back at one o'clock. The square is packed with fifty thousand people. The secretary is so far away he can't even see the balcony. The crowd cheers. There's a Yankee tourist standing near by with a pair of field-glasses. The secretary begs him: "Lend me your field-glasses." The Yank says: "They're not field-glasses, they're binoculars. And you can't borrow them. I've come ten thousand miles to see the Vatican . . ." The secretary says: "Well, what can you see?" "Two men standing on the balcony," the Yank tells him. The secretary tugs his arm. "Can you recognise them? Who are they?" The Yank takes a good look through his binoculars: "Well, I can't place the guy in the funny hat but the other guy is definitely Dooley Franks from Parramatta."

Excerpt from 'Yarns of Billy Borker' by Frank Hardy published by A. H. & A. W. Reed

Horne, Williams & Paddick.

bona ballet

Horne So you're the Ballet Bona now?

Julian Yes. I'm Julinski and this is my friend, Sandeyev.

Sandy Well, how nice to vada your eek again, Mr. Horne. What brings you trolling in here?

Horne I heard you were presenting a new ballet. Could you tell me something about it?

Julian Yes – it's called *L'Apres-midi d'un Goose.*

Sandy That is your actual French, with the exception of goose, and we don't know the French for that. It means your goose's afternoon. That is the actual translation, isn't it, Jule?

Julian Yes That is your actual –

Sandy Translation.

Julian Yes. You see, we're bilingual. We've been suivezing la piste on the telly every Friday. Does wonders for your bon mots.

Horne Why goose?

Sandy Why not?

Horne Well, surely it should be *L'Apres-midi d'un Faun.*

Sandy Well, you see, we went up the costumiers but they didn't have no fauns' costumes left. All they had was a goose left over from panto. It's actually got a trapdoor in it for dropping your golden egg out of, but we're not using that. It lacks poetry – among other things.

Julian 'Course, the big drawback is that it's a second-hand goose, you see. I mean, you don't know who's been in there. Still, you have to suffer for your art, don't you?

Horne Well, what actually is the story of the ballet?

Sandy Well, you see, Jule here is the Goose King and I'm a hunter –Prince Roderick the Mighty. And I'm trolling through the forest one day and I come across this lovely creature –

Julian That's me.

Sandy He looks better in the skin. So anyway, I vada this goose cruising about on this magic pool. So what happens? I'll tell you what happens – all me hunting instincts rise, and I whip out me crossbow, do a pas de chat all around the stage, very butch-like, then I take aim and fire – and transfix him with me magic barb. Then he does the Dance of the Dying Goose.

Horne I'd like to see him. Do you think he'd do it for me now?

Sandy Ask him, ducky.

Horne Would you die for me?

Julian Gladly.

Sandy There he goes. He's dying now. Look at him flapping away. Flap, flap, flap, go on, gel! Oh, it's very pathetic, isn't it?

Horne You took the word right out of my mouth.

Julian *(grunts and groans as he prances about)*

Sandy There he goes – he's going now – it's ebbing away. No wait a minute, it's coming back. No, he's going again, look, look – the way he's all curled up in a little ball – ah, bless him.

Julian *(bellows with pain).*

Sandy What's up?

Julian I've got me beak caught up me trapdoor. Hang on a minute. Right. Now, with a final flutter of my broken wings, I stagger back to the magic pool and plunge in.

Sandy Filled with remorse. I leap into the pool after him and after a breathtaking pas de deux, we expire together. The whole denouement smacks more than a little of the definitely fantabulosa.

Julian 'Course, we know that we're a little far out. We're only on the fringe, as it were.

Horne Of the festival?

Julian Oh, yes. *And* of the festival. But if we get the critical acclaim we deserve, it'll mean a world tour – Monte Carlo, the Lincoln Centre, the Bolshoi, Covent Garden –

Horne And if it doesn't succeed?

Sandy Well, I s'pose it's back to washing up at the Corner House.

Excerpt from 'The Bona Book of Julian and Sandy' by Barry Took and Marty Feldman published by Robson Books Ltd.

Holy Snaps

PLAYBOY
Feldman's
Album of Carols
Feldman's
Album of Carols

VIEWS OF THE WORLD

SHY VICAR SNAPS

Before a congregation of some 120, the Reverend Clifford Lacey of St. John's, Eltham, began the nuptials of Rosemary Nicholson and David Mullett — a former choirboy.

The words "Dearly Beloved . . ." had scarcely passed the Reverend Lacey's lips when the bride's brother nipped out from behind the pulpit and panned across the faithful with his cine-camera, finishing the shot with a close-up of the verger, George Tubby, aged 72, a veteran of two world wars.

Reverend Lacey told Mr Nicholson to clear off; Mr Nicholson refused; whereupon, to the amazement of the devout, a shouting match developed between them, to which Mr Harry Nicholson, the bride's father, soon added his voice.

The Reverend Lacey said that he had not given permission to photograph the choirgirls.

Leading schoolgirl Anne Butterbub said: "I feel sorry for the happy couple."

"Get on with it", said the bride's father, "he's not using lights."

Towards the end of the ceremony, a bagpiper dressed in a kilt walked down the aisle playing *Amazing Grace*. This disturbed the organist, Mr Beam, who played the theme from *Dr Zhivago* (the bride's personal request) all the louder.

Later, in the vestry, there was, according to the Vicar, "some jostling".

The bride's father, a retired paratrooper, said: "If the Queen can have her wedding on film, so can Rosemary" — and challenged the Reverend Lacey to a fight. Several wedding guests began to dance among the graves, and, when Mr Tubby thrust his offertory plate towards them, it was knocked into the air.

"The bagpiper is a relative", shouted Mr Nicholson. "This do cost me a tenner, and I've thrown it away."

Mr Tubby said: "I've done a couple of hundred of these in the last few months, but this one beats the lot. I was abused by the majority of the guests, and all I got for the job was 50p."

Mr Nicholson, the bride's father, has written a letter of complaint to the Archbishop of Canterbury.

After sentencing a man to 1,500 years for rape the judge said that it struck him as a reasonable punishment. "500 years would have been just a slap on the wrist."

Suit goes for a Burton

Mr Bejoy Khar came from Pakistan to Birmingham.

Each week he put aside a little of his earnings. He was saving for a summer suit.

"I even kept myself short of food," he said.

Eventually he had the right amount — £30; he collected his suit and put it carefully away.

In May Mr Khar went south for his annual holiday. The following day he took his suit out of its cellophane wrapping and walked in its elegance beside the river Wye.

He had covered no more than a hundred yards when he saw a small dog struggling for its life in the river. Mr Khar leapt in to save it.

"Not till I was in mid-air did I remember my suit," he said.

He landed on a bank of deep black slime.

The dog, annoyed at having its swim disturbed, gave Mr Khar a nasty bite and swam ashore wagging its tail.

"The funny thing is, I don't really like dogs," said Mr Khar.

Suits off the Peg

Mr Harvey Stippleton, a Berkshire shoplifter, claimed that he had carried seven suits out of Harrod's store to compare them in the light.

On being reminded that he was shopping after five o'clock on a January evening, Stippleton said that he had forgotten about double summer time.

CAVITY RADIO

Shortly after visiting her dentist, a housewife of Daytona Beach, Florida was awakened in the middle of the nght by her husband who complained that her teeth were broadcasting. He was right.

Her dentist, Dr. John Long, explained that certain metallic fillings when contacted by acidulous saliva can create a receiving set.

"it will pass off in a few days," he said. "Meantime keep your mouth closed as much as you can, for its natural cavity forms an effective baffle box, thereby increasing the volume."

The lady did as she was told and the broadcasts ceased. "I thought I was free of the trouble and ready to throw a party," she said. "But no sooner were things under way than I opened my mouth to laugh and out came the theme song from *Doctor Zhivago* followed by *Rambling Rose*. Fortunately our friends are all broadminded. Some of them even danced to the tunes."

A Man's Best Friend

Answering a charge of cruelty against his dog Prince, Mr Sean Wilby assurred the court that he did not intend to hurt the animal when he bit it.

"Prince and I do a trick together," he said. "When I go: "Gerrh!" "Gerrh!" Prince crouches down. When I shout: "Oops!" Prince jumps up in the air and I catch him in my mouth.

"To describe it as cruel is nonsense. I do the same with children."

CHAMPION FROGS IN DEAD HEAT

Disaster overtook both finalists in this year's Mark Twain Memorial Frog-Jumping Tournament, held in the writer's home at Hartford, Connecticut.

Fierce preliminary contests left two Iowa frogs, "Beadle" of Sioux City and "Big Dick" of Oskaloosa, deadlocked with matching 87-inch three jump totals.

In order to get a clear decision the rule forbidding physical encouragement by owner was waived.

"Beadle", spurred by a slap on the jumping table, managed 66 inches in two jumps, but died of a heart attack on landing; while "Big Dick", after his owner fired a starting pistol, leapt off the table into the mouth of "Sunny", a guard dog used for patrolling the literary shrine at night.

WILD LIFE — MAN SHOT

Darius Giraud, an ornithologist from Toulon, spent many hours in learning how to imitate the cries of rare birds. While practising in the woods near his home he was shot and killed by a hunter.

Typical Conservative

A convention of eunuchs has been called at the Sukkur, 315 miles north of Karachi, to decide on their policy for the next general election in Pakistan. A spokesman for the eunuchs said: "We are typical conservative voters. We see no need for change."

ARTY FACTS

Does it still linger somewhere, I wonder, the idea of the artist as a romantic bohemian, roaming free and living it up? The Victorians, of course, played it up like mad — long hair, wild colours, sex galore and a gaggle of barefoot children belonging to heaven knows who — even the mothers weren't too sure which were theirs. It must have been very tiring to keep that sort of thing going — when what you really wanted was somewhere warm with no holes in the roof, one man at a time, and some regular cash to eat regular meals on. Heaven (and the artist) knows it's not particularly funny — even in these grants for the boys-and-girls days — to persuade enough people that your picture/book/song/statue/bit of old bent wire is actually worth **paying** *for. Bohemian old clothes, forget it.*

At least, I think that's how the artist sees it. The few **real** *ones I know (and there are plenty of phonies about with more than a touch of the Augustus Johns) may wear fairly old clothes, but they're old-respectable not old-tatty. In fact, the first time a poet called on me, I thought he was the man come to read the meter.*

K.B.

BORGE & HOFFNUNG ON MUSIC

WAGNER

Richard Wagner wore pink underwear, climbed trees, and liked to stand on his head, but right side up he wrote some nice music. Did you know that in Italian the word "opera" means "works"? Wagner did, and when you go to any of his operas, that's just what you get.

First Impressions

As a boy I heard most of them when my father, who was a member of the Royal Opera House Orchestra in Copenhagen, took me with him to the rehearsals. I would sit there for hours, listening to the arias, all of which were translated, probably because the singers couldn't pronounce all those complicated German words. They couldn't always pronounce them in Danish either, but at least it didn't take so long. I remember my first Wagner opera well. By the time Tannhauser had reached the Venusberg, I had reached the streetcar on my way home. It had become quite clear to me what Rossini meant when he said that Wagner had some fine moments, but terrible quarter-hours.

Tristan and Isolde, is a plain everyday tale of jealousy, treachery, sorcery, passion, remorse, anguish, betrayal, death, murder, and love. Actually, it has everything in it but a Wedding March, and that's only because Wagner had just used up his best one for *Lohengrin.* Isolde is an Irish Princess who claims to hate Tristan except we know better, and Tristan is a Cornish Knight who is taking her to England to marry King Mark to whom he claims to be terribly devoted. Except we know better about that, too. Since Isolde would rather die than marry Mark, she decides to share a Death Potion with Tristan and get the opera over with. Now it might have worked, and for once we might really have wound up with a Wagner special that doesn't last all night. But no. Isolde sends Brangane to get the potion. Brangane is Isolde's Lady-in-Waiting, and she's been waiting around during the whole opera, with hardly anything to do but bring the Death Potion, and she can't even do that right. She brings in a Love Potion instead. Next thing you know, Tristan and Isolde are embracing each other passionately, and another two hours are shot.

In the Second Act, Isolde has married King Mark anyway, but you couldn't tell it without a program. As soon as the King goes off hunting, Isolde signals Tristan, and there they are again, embracing each other passionately, and singing tender love duets at the top of their lungs. Alas. Of all days, the King picks that one to get home early, and he catches Tristan and Isolde smack in the middle of a leitmotif. Furiously jealous, because he doesn't have much to do in the opera either, he sends in one of his soldiers to cross swords with Tristan. Tristan adores cross-sword puzzles, but this time he gets wounded immediately, because his mind is still back in the love duet.

In the last act, Tristan is on a cot, peacefully suffering, when he learns that Isolde is coming to visit him. Obviously he can't take that sort of news lying down, so he gets up and sings another love song. Unfortunately, the strain is too much for him, and just as Isolde enters, he dies of the sword wounds in her arms. A couple of others enter and get killed too, and finally Isolde dies her famous Love Death. I guess it isn't a barrel of laughs. But it does contain some of the most radiant music in all opera, which is something.

BERLIOZ

The life of Hector Berlioz is recommended for mature adults only, although no one would dare make a movie out of it. Berlioz lived right in the middle of the romantic era, and he didn't forget it for a minute. "My arteries quiver violently", he wrote in his *Memoirs,* "my muscles contract spasmodically, my limbs tremble, my feet and hands go numb." That was from listening to music. Wait till you hear what happened when he found out about girls.

Igor Straveinsky wrote an Elephant Polka and brought a copy to the Metropolitan Opera. The Met wanted no part of it. They had enough trouble cleaning up after the horses in Wagner's *Die Walkure.* So Stravinsky took the polka to the Ringling Brothers' Circus. The Ringling Brothers at first were doubtful, too. They thought the tune was OK, but they didn't care for the choreography much. It just didn't ringle the bell. Fortunately, they called in George Balanchine, and before long he fixed up some much better steps for the elephants.

The Piccolo Double Bass

The Harp

Basic Training

After that, the main problem was teaching the steps to the corps de ballet. Whoever started that rumour about elephants never forgetting should have been there. They were forgetting all over the place. Balanchine would explain a step to the elephants over and over again, and what happened? The next morning, all they could remember was how to walk around the ring chomping on each other's tails. Finally, opening night arrived, and Balanchine was so nervous that he rushed out and hired a couple of ballerinas for safety's sake, just in case the elephants forgot their parts again. But they didn't. The Circus Polka was a hit, and it marked an important turning point in Stravinsky's career. It was the last time he ever wrote anything for elephants.

Operettas are just like operas, only not so much. Sometimes they are called light operas, because they're shorter and the prima donnas weigh less.

The very first comic opera was composed in 1639 by two Italians named Mazzocchi and Marazzoli, which was enough to start anybody laughing. Giulio Rospigliosi, who wrote the libretto, was so ashamed of himself that he gave up the theatre and joined the church. Eventually, he became Pope Clement IX. How repentant can you get?

Words from 'My Favourite Intervals' by Victor Borge published by The Woburn Press. Pictures from The Hoffnung Symphony Orchestra by Gerard Hoffnung Published by Dobson Books Ltd.

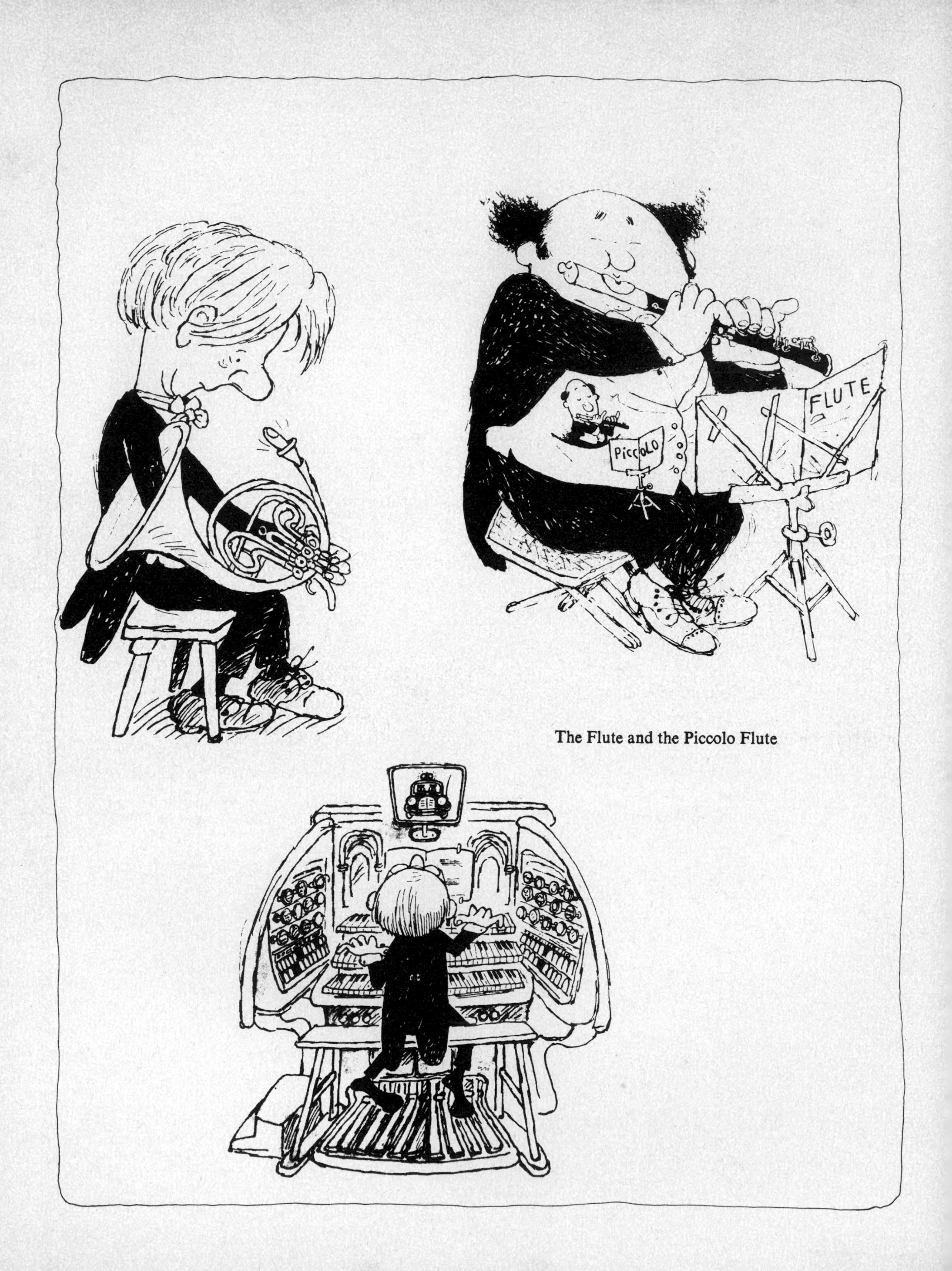

The Flute and the Piccolo Flute

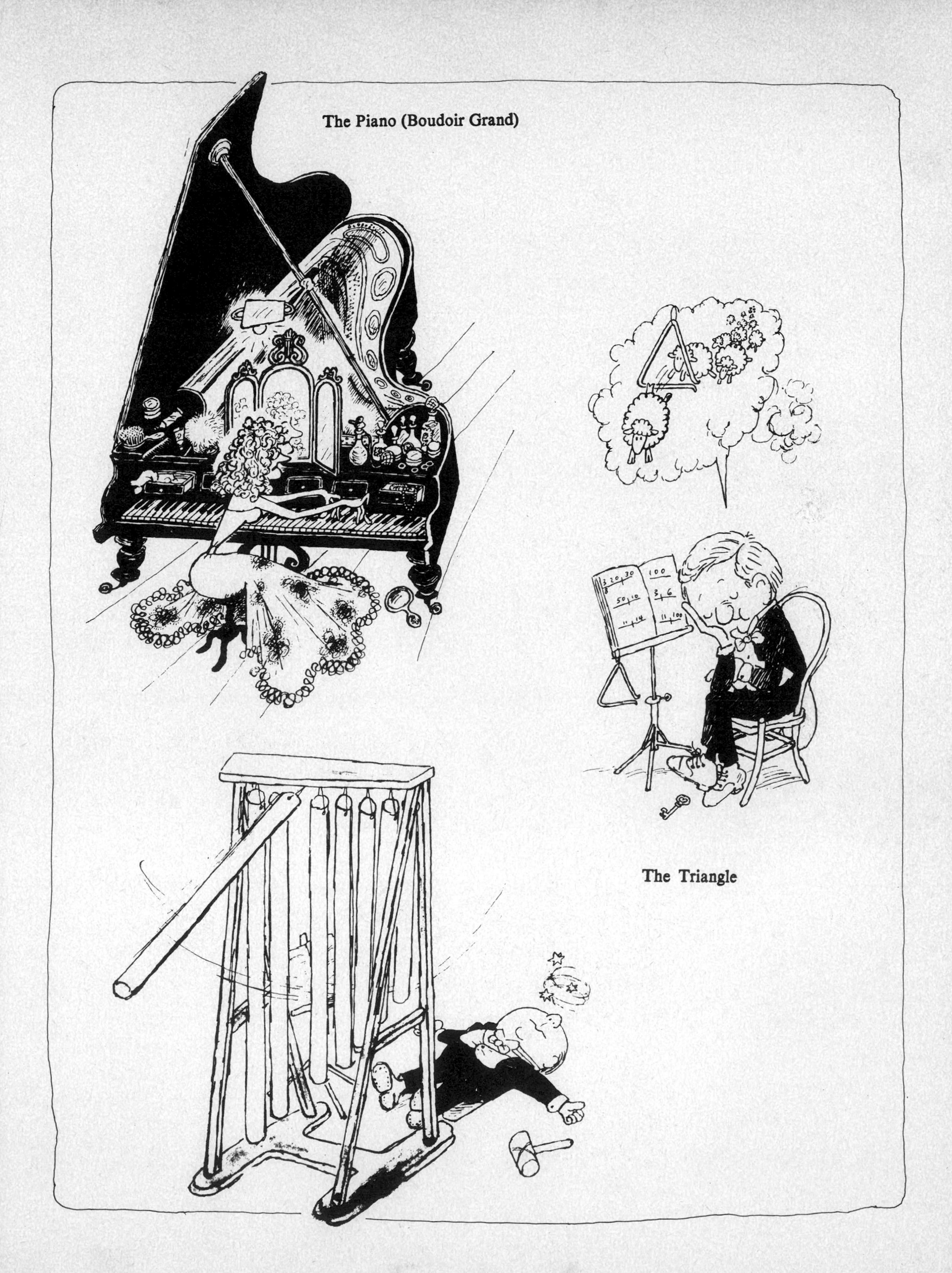

The Piano (Boudoir Grand)

The Triangle

In Other Words

A maiden at college named Breeze,
Weighed down by B.A.'s and Litt.D.'s,
Collapsed from the strain.
Alas, it was plain
She was killing herself by degrees.

I sat next to the Duchess at tea;
It was just as I feared it would be:
Her rumblings abdominal
Were truly phenomenal,
And everyone thought it was me!

There was a young fellow named Sydney
Who drank till he ruined his kidney.
It shriveled and shrank
As he sat there and drank,
But he had a good time at it, didn't he?

The Marquis de Sade and Genet
Are most highly thought of today;
But torture and treachery
Are not my sort of lechery,
So I've given my copies away.

There's a notable family named Stein,
There's Gertrude, there's Ep, and there's Ein.
Gert's prose is the bunk,
Ep's sculpture is junk,
And no one can understand Ein!

A buxom young typist named Baynes
At her work took particular pains.
She was good at dictation
And long explanations,
But she ran more to bosom than brains.

There was a young man with a hernia
Who said to his doctor, 'Goldernia,
When improving my middle
Be sure you don't fiddle
With matters that do not concernia.'

There was a young priest named Delane
Who said to the girls, 'Nota bene,
'Twould tempt the archbishop
The way that you swish up
Your skirts when the weather is rainy.'

There was a young man of Bengal
Who went to a masquerade ball
Arrayed like a tree,
But he failed to foresee
His abuse by the dogs in the hall.

A sensitive lady from Worcester
At a ball met a fellow who gorcester;
A lecherous guy
With blood in his uy,
So she ducked out before he sedorcester.

Rosalina, a pretty young lass
Had a truly magnificent ass:
Not rounded and pink,
As you possible think
It was grey, had long ears, and ate grass.

A wanton young lady of Wimley,
Reproached for not acting more primly,
Answered, 'Heavens above!
I know sex isn't love,
But it's such an attractive facsimile.'

There was a young warrior of Parma
Who got into bed with his charma.
She, naturally nude,
Said, 'Don't think me rude,
But I do wish you'd take off your arma!

There was an old lady of Harrow
Whose views were exceedingly narrow.
At the end of her paths
She built two bird baths
For the different sexes of sparrow.

from

David Niven

Bring on the Empty Horses

At Christmas 1947 I gave a party for my two small sons and Tyrone Power offered to play Santa Claus. 'Ty' was everybody's favourite person and all agreed that he was that great rarity—a man who was just as nice as he seemed to be. With his flashing good looks, graceful carriage and easy laughter, it was no surprise that he was a Pied Piper to women—they followed him in droves wherever he went—but 'Ty' was a simple person, with a great down-to-earthness and modesty about himself. He lived a few blocks from me and I went over to help him dress and brief him on the impending operation.

He was extremely nervous.

'This is worse than a first night on Broadway,' he said, helping himself liberally to the Scotch bottle. 'I've never performed for a bunch of kids before.'

I pushed and pulled him into the padded stomach, bulky red outfit and high black boots rented from Western Costume Company and helped him fasten on a black belt, a huge white beard and little red cap.

'Don't worry about it,' I said, 'it's all fixed. I've left the gate open at the bottom of the garden. I've rigged up some sleigh bells down there and stashed away the presents, and at exactly six o'clock we'll give 'em the bells, then you pick up the sack and make it up the lawn to the house — they're all expecting you.'

'Oh God!' 'Ty' groaned. 'Why the hell did I suggest this? — hand me that bottle.'

Another hefty swig passed through the cotton-wool beard.

'Whose kids are they anyway?' he asked.

'Two of mine, Maria Cooper, Ros Russell's kid, the Fairbanks' and Deborah's, Loretta's and Jerry Lewis', Michael Boyer, and Edgar Bergen's little girl "Candy", about fifty all together. You'll know a lot of them, the rest are neighbours.'

'Fifty!!' yelled 'Ty' . . . 'hand me that bottle.'

'Don't worry,' I said, 'I've written all the names clearly on each present; just read 'em out . . . ad lib a little and don't forget to go HO! HO! HO!'

'Jesus!' said 'Ty'. 'Let's go . . . I can't stand all this waiting around.'

One last nip and we were off; we took the bottle along.

During the five-minute drive to my house 'Ty' begged me to let him off the hook.

'Why don't *you* do it?' he asked. 'It's your party.'

'You suggested it,' I said firmly.

By six o'clock, Santa Claus was loaded in every sense of the word and, sack on shoulder, was hidden in some bushes at the bottom of my garden.

I tugged the string and pealed the sleigh bells.

Immediately, excited cries broke out from the house and little heads appeared at every window.

'Off you go,' I said to my quivering companion. 'Lots of luck!'

'Son of a *Bitch!*' hissed Father Christmas and lurched off up the lawn.

When his shadowy form was spotted by the excited children, shrill shrieks and applause broke out. At that point I had intended to turn on the garden lights to illuminate the scene, but for some reason I missed the switch and turned on the sprinklers. With a crack! like a pistol shot, geysers of spray shot out of the grass all around him and 'Ty' fell down. I readjusted the situation;

'Ty' picked himself up, gave me a marked look, and squelched on towards the shining, expectant faces in the windows.

Like all actors, once the curtain was up and the adrenalin had started pumping, 'Ty' was relaxed and happy in his work. 'HO! HO! HO!' he boomed, 'and *who* is this lovely woolly lamb for, eh?' (fumbling at the card).

'Aha! I remember now . . . Candice Bergen! Come here, little girl . . . HO! HO! HO!'

He was doing beautifully by the time I had sneaked in by the back door . . . seated in a big chair in the hall with excited children climbing all over him.

'And who is *this* gentleman?' he asked my eldest son, indicating me.

'That's my Daddy,' the little boy piped up.

'Well now . . . I wonder if your Daddy could spare old Santa a glass of iemonade . . . I've come a *long* way tonight.'

A sizeable belt of Scotch disappeared into the white foliage and 'Ty' became too sure of himself.

'Maria Cooper! . . . *My!* what a pretty girl! HO! HO! HO! you tell your Daddy that old Santa

thought he was just dandy in *High Noon* . . . and ask him for Grace Kelly's phone number while you're about it . . . HO! HO! HO!'

Maria Cooper was a little more sophisticated than the other children.

'Where did you see the picture, Santa?' she asked sweetly.

'Oh,' said 'Ty', pointing vaguely above him . . . 'up there!'

After a while, Santa made his goodbyes and staggered off down the lawn: some of the children cried when he left, one complained about his breath.

Back at the bottom of the garden, I helped him out of his outfit: he was as excited as if he had just given a triumphant Broadway performance of *King Lear*. 'I really enjoyed that!' he said, 'weren't the kids a *great* audience!!'

Up at the house he mingled unnoticed with arriving parents and was beside me when my youngest son emerged from a bedroom flushed with embarrassment.

'Daddy! Daddy! guess *what?* That Candy Bergen has been trying to *kiss* me.'

Some Hollywood children *never* knew when they were well off.

Errol Flynn once utilised a favourite Hollywood 'ploy' on a pompous Washington diplomat who was pestering him for an invitation to a 'real' Hollywood party. The man arrived at the appointed hour and was delighted when a gorgeous maid wearing nothing but shoes, stockings and a little white cap opened the door.

'The undressing room is here, sir,' she said, indicating a room full of discarded clothing.

'When you are ready, sir, I'll take you in to the party.' She smiled seductively.

The man soon appeared naked, his eyes shining with excitement.

'I hope you'll have some fun, sir,' said the maid, 'follow me, please.'

He did, appreciating the sway of her hips and her twinkling behind.

She stopped at a door. The sound of revelry came from within. She asked his name, opened the door and announced it. The diplomat charged in like a bull at a corrida.

Thirty people in full evening dress looked at him disapprovingly.

FIVE HOURS BACK

We are here to escape from Religious Persecution — What are you here for?

The nice thing about America is that it's everthing we are, only more so—sometimes much more so. Alright, so we've got barbequed chicken flavour potato crisps which seem pretty unbelievable to me—but in the States, would you believe, they've got T-shirts—sold by **Smell It Like It Is** *Inc.—which are (wait for it) impregnated with perfumes which are activated by body-heat. Among the 200 smells on offer are banana, pine, orange, beer, cold lamb and Kentucky fried chicken. And if you wrote to the company, asking why no mint sauce with the cold lamb, you know what they'd do? They'd add it, that's what—and probably send you a free cold-lamb-and-mint-sauce T-shirt as well.*

And just to prove that the Americans themselves think they're funny, I asked an American (Angele Ritter of 20th Century Fox, Hollywood) to send me the material for the following all-American pages. *K.B.*

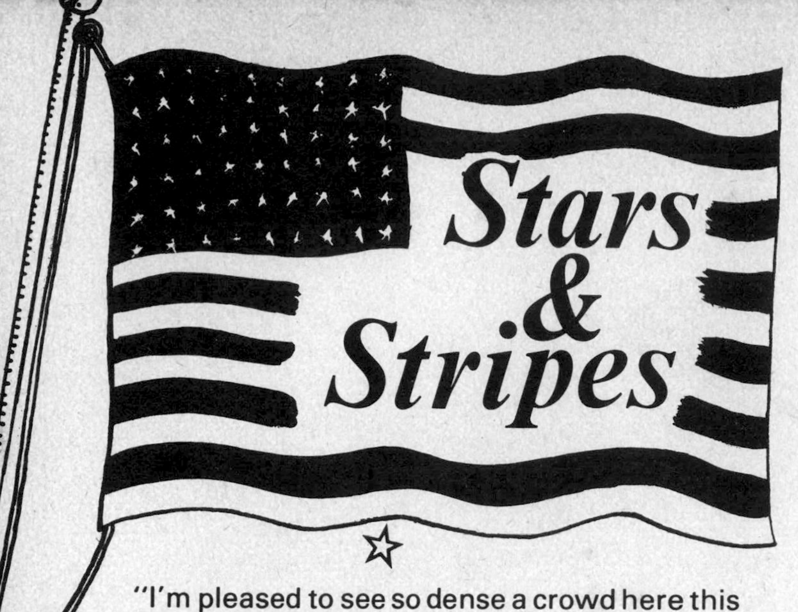

"I'm pleased to see so dense a crowd here this evening," said the politician as he began his speech.

"Don't be too sure of yourself, mister," cried out one man. "We ain't as dense as you think."

Frank Sinatra persuaded golf expert Arnold Palmer to play eighteen holes with him at Palm Springs one morning. The round completed, Sinatra asked anxiously, "What do you think of my game?" "Not bad," conceded Palmer, "but I still prefer golf."

A New Englander horse trader sold a pair of horses which he guaranteed were willing horses. Shortly afterwards the buyer complained that the horses were very poor workers. "You told me that these horses were willing."

"So I did," said the seller. "And they are willing. One is willing to stop, and the other is willing to let him."

Overheard in the Beauty Parlor.

"I knew he couldn't be trusted. He has gone back to his wife".

"I see so little of him, I feel like I took his name in vain".

An incorrigible old reprobate of eighty-six consulted his doctor before taking unto himself a sultry bride of twenty-one. "Marry her if you must", said the doctor dubiously, "but restrain yourself. Overexertion could well prove fatal". The reprobate shrugged his shoulders and philosophized, "Well, if she dies, she dies".

'AT LAST, A MOVIE WITHOUT ALL THOSE FILTHY SEX SCENES'

The small town was shaken to its foundations by a political question. When one of the town's sages was asked for his opinion, he said, "I haven't yet decided which side I'm on. But I'll tell you this: When I do make up my mind I'm goin' to be damn bitter about it!"

"I want a tooth pulled," an imperious lady told a Cape Cod dentist, "and I don't want any anaesthetic, because I'm in a hurry." Impressed with her bravery, the good doctor asked which tooth it was. "Donald," said the lady, turning to her husband, "show him your tooth."

FORM USA 123

TAXES SPELL TEXAS

Taxes are taxes wherever you pay them – or try to avoid paying them – and it hurts just as much and Americans work as hard as we do to smile as they cough up their hard-earned cash.

Here are a few personal messages found on their income-tax returns:

Gentlemen:
Why don't you simplify the form? Just ask:
Whadja make? Whadja spend?
Whadja got left? Send it in!

I'm telling you guys for the last time! My wife's relatives *are* an organized charity.

"Gentlemen, I have not been able to sleep nights account of worrying about not having reported on a good deal of income. So I'm enclosing my check for $1,000. If I find I still can't sleep, I'll send the rest of it".

A family corporation wanted to charge off the cost of a 'water purification experiment' which investigators found to be the family swimming pool at their summer home.

A stock-market operator wanted to deduct the cost of fees paid to an astrologer for market guidance.

A man who listed as a charitable contribution the cost of a tombstone over his brother's grave was asked by Internal Revenue to explain this. He said that since his brother never did anything for him, the erection of the tombstone was an act of charity.

The Bureau of Internal Revenue received a typed income tax return from a bachelor, who had listed one dependent. The examiner returned it with a notation: "This must be a stenographic error".

"You're telling me", the taxpayer answered in writing after the pencilled notation.

ONE UP ON WEBSTER

from Bennett Cerf's private dictionary

Abalone: An expression of disbelief.
Bigamist: Fog over Naples.
Bulldozer: One who sleeps through campaign speeches.
Buttress: A female goat.
Croquette: Romantic lady frog.
Debate: What attracts de fish.
Escalator: Stairway to the stores.
Hangover: The wrath of grapes.
Lawyer: A man who sees to it that you get what's coming to him.
Nudist Colony: A retreat where men and women go to air their differences.
Recession: A time when we have to do without a lot of things our grandparents never heard of.
Sore Throat: Hoarse and buggy.
Vice Versa: Poetry not fit for the kiddies to read.
Well Informed: A person whose opinions are the same as yours.

Excerpt from 'Sound of Laughter' by Bennett Cerf, Doubleday & Co. N.Y.

You can take it from me (and I've lived there) there are no squares in Hollywood – but some funny people play a very funny quiz game on T.V. called . . . .

Hollywood Squares

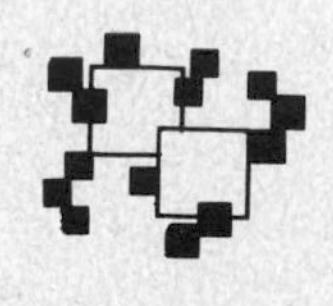

In doing traditional yoga exercises, when a person crosses his legs, entwines them under him, and tucks his heels up in his groin, what's it called?
Charley Weaver: It's still called his groin, but it looks different.

■

Is bowling big in Japan?
Lily Tomlin: *Nothing* is big in Japan.

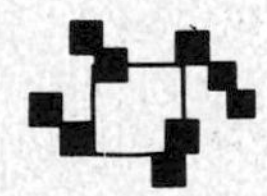

What did it mean in the 16th century when a woman slept with a milk-soaked veal cutlet on each cheek?
Marty Allen: Same as it does today, . . . She's bananas.

■

In mythology, Alexander the Great finally cut the legendary Gordian Knot. Then what happened?
Charley Weaver: Gordian's pants fell down.

■

According to Greek mythology, the god, Apollo, in love with the maiden, Daphne, pursued her through the forest. When he caught her, what did she change into?
Mel Brooks: Something comfortable.

■

Louisa May Alcott wrote the famous book, *Little Women.* She also wrote a book about men. What was it called?
Paul Lynde: **What you Always Wanted to Know About Little Women But Were Afraid to Ask.**

When the Lone Ranger was finished with a case, he left something behind. What?
Paul Lynde: **A masked baby.**

■

Just before he starts milking, there's one thing a good farmer does. What?
Charley Weaver: Makes sure it's a cow.

■

On the average, how much does your liver weigh?
Charley Weaver: **Twice as much as my onions.**

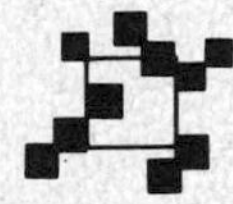

According to the famous quote by Alexander Pope, a little *what* is a dangerous thing?
Paul Lynde: **A little pervert.**

■

Every night your wife covers her face with yogurt. Is that beneficial?
Charley Weaver: It helps, but I can still tell it's her.

■

True or false: It's against the law in New York to sell alligator shoes?
Rose Marie: **You can't sell them drinks, either.**

■

True or false: The ancient Chinese believed intense romantic encounters caused toothaches?
Paul Lynde: **Well then, the ancient Chinese did it wrong!**

HAVING A BABY CAN BE A SCREAM

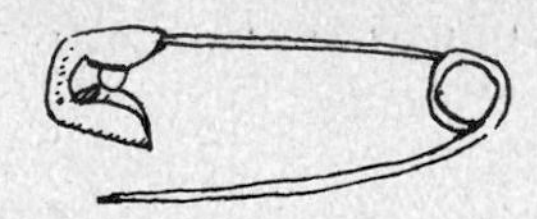

by JOAN RIVERS

When my husband, Edgar, and I were courting, he said he couldn't wait to have a baby. It was only after we were married that he changed his mind and decided that I should have the baby. And that's when I got frightened.

Like most women, I had always wanted children, but when my rabbit finally died I was fraught with questions. Was I ready to become a mother? Did I know enough? Would the baby and I survive my amateur bumblings? And did the rabbit leave a will? Well, I was, I did, we have, and he didn't.

And that's why I am writing this. To let every pregnant woman (and man) out there know that you can smile your way in and out of the maternity ward. And all through motherhood, too. Well, almost.

Having a baby and becoming a mother should be a ball. Not a bawl. And yet throughout history women have passed down such tales of horror to each other ("I was in labor 108 days". "My doctor left more stitches in me than in an entire knit dress". "They had to give me gas, plus a spinal, plus ether — and I still felt everything!") that almost every pregnant woman approaches the big event with fear and trepidation.

Six years ago I was almost one of them. I was scared silly. Mainly because my cousin Shirley, who never complains, screamed and screamed when she was having her baby. True, this was just during *conception*. But it put me off.

So I started asking around exactly what was what. I called and interviewed dozens of obstetricians, pediatricians and one chiropodist by mistake. I started asking them questions, questions, questions. Each one kindly gave me answers, answers, answers. (Except one obstetrician, who in order to avoid me moved to China and is now delivering babies by acupuncture).

Mainly because of these conversations, and the knowledge that I acquired from them, when my big Day came (January 20, 1968), it was joyous and exciting — and well worth the minor pain and discomfort I suffered when I broke two front teeth while biting down on a bullet . . .

To help prepare myself for the blessed event, I exercised all through pregnancy, even though it looked silly. Did you ever see a bunch of pregnant women running around a gym? We looked like a volleyball game where every player had the ball.

I also took a natural childbirth course. It was terrific. They used to put all of us pregnant mommies into gym suits and lay us down on the gym floor to do our exercises. We looked like a relief map of the Rocky Mountains. They explained everything that would happen during labor. At the end, they even showed a movie of a woman giving birth to her baby. I enjoyed that part the most. But for some reason, they threw me out of class. Maybe it was because I asked them to run the movie backward. "Come on, nurse", I shouted, "now let's see the baby disappear".

The first thing that really got me crazy about Melissa (*the baby*) was the amount of food she could put away. And what got me even crazier was that it went in one end and immediately out the other. Things went through her so fast that I figured the wisest thing I could do was to feed her on the potty.

But, I let her enjoy herself. After all, I figured she was taking after my side of the family. I have a cousin Shirley who eats like the Cossacks are in Newark. She once stayed over at my house. The next day I couldn't believe the amount of food she put away — 4 pizzas, 5 quarts of milk, 2 loaves of bread, 2 fried chickens and a pint of tuti-frutti ice cream. And that was just for breakfast!

Watching Melissa eat gave me a lot of pleasure for two reasons. One, I figured she really was enjoying herself, and two, she was still too young to realize what a terrible cook I am. Bad cooking runs in my family but who cares? We've all survived. My mother, for example, was a terrible cook. For the first ten years of my life I was brought up on radio dinners. Then she switched to TV dinners. Mother would stand over us and insist we eat them, and boy they tasted horrible — she never warmed them up.

Excerpt published by Toni Mendez Inc.

ADVERTISING (wrote Stephen Leacock) may be described as the science of arresting the human intelligence long enough to get money from it.

★

A stout-hearted fellow, tired of doing undercover work for the espionage department of a country we won't identify, applied for a post with a Madison Avenue advertising agency. The job application blank included the question, "What qualifications do you have?" Whimsically, the applicant wrote, "Spying, arson, burglary, kidnapping, etc." Furthermore, he got the job.

A year or so later, combing the files, he came across his personnel folder. On his job application form, a top executive had written, "This fellow obviously is one of us. Grab him!"

★

Faith will never die so long as colored seed catalogs are printed.

An Arkansas salesman of advertising space called on a small town merchant who said, "Nothing doing. I've been established for forty years and never advertised."

As he turned to leave the salesman asked, "What is that building on the hill?"

"Oh, that's the local church."

"Been there long?"

"A hundred years or so."

"Well, they still ring the bell," said the salesman.

★

George Martin said hair-restorer ads were "a lot of balderdash."

★

And I want to tell you (says Phyllis Diller)
About the world's most fabulous new cosmetic.
It's a new odor-under-de-armament.
And the name of it is *Whisht!*
And it's so great,
It works on an entirely different principle.
It doesn't kill the odor at all.
Just makes you invisible —
And nobody can figure out
Who smells!

★

Advertising: Something which makes one think he's longed all his life for a thing he never even heard of before.

★

When Mark Twain was editor of a small-town paper, he received a letter from an old subscriber, complaining that he had found a spider in his paper and asking whether this was a sign of good or bad luck. Mark Twain replied:

"Dear Old Subscriber: Finding a spider in your paper was neither good luck nor bad luck for you. The spider was merely looking over our paper to see which merchant is not advertising, so that he can go to that store, spin his web across the door, and lead a life of undisturbed peace ever afterward."

Two local dairies engaged in an advertising war. One hired a daredevil driver to drive a car around town with a large placard reading: THIS DAREDEVIL DRINKS OUR MILK.

The rival company came out with a larger sign reading: YOU DON'T HAVE TO BE A DAREDEVIL TO DRINK OUR MILK.

SIGNS OF THE (AMERICAN) TIMES

Sidewalker-vendor sign on tomatoes: DON'T SQUEEZE ME UNTIL I'M YOURS.

Note left on the door of a music store: JOHANN TO LUNCH. BACH AT ONE. OFFENBACH SOONER.

Sign in bar: STAY A WHILE LONGER, YOUR WIFE CAN ONLY GET SO MAD.

Notice outside a Chicago print shop: MARRIAGES ARE MADE IN HEAVEN, BUT WE PRINT THE INVITATIONS.

Outside a loan company branch: "WE'RE HERE FOR THE MAN WHO ALREADY HAS EVERYTHING — BUT HASN'T PAID FOR IT".

Pawnshop notice: PLEASE SEE ME AT YOUR EARLIEST INCONVENIENCE.

Sign in a shop window: OUR CLOTHES NOT ONLY MAKE GIRLS LOOK SLIM, THEY ALSO MAKE MEN LOOK ROUND.

Sign in optometrist's window: IF YOU DON'T SEE WHAT YOU WANT, YOU'VE COME TO THE RIGHT PLACE.

In a restaurant: IT'S TOUGH TO PAY TWO DOLLARS FOR A STEAK. BUT IT'S TOUGHER WHEN YOU PAY ONE DOLLAR.

On a self-service elevator: "EIGHTH FLOOR BUTTON OUT OF ORDER. PLEASE PUSH FIVE AND THREE".

Near Woodlawn Cemetry: "Second-hand tomb-stone for sale. Extraordinary bargain for family named Schwarzendorfer".

The new pedestrian lights in Las Vegas are marked. "STOP", "GO", and "THREE TO ONE YOU DON'T MAKE IT".

At cash desk in Miami restaurant: IF YOU ARE OVER 80 AND ACCOMPANIED BY YOUR PARENTS, WE WILL CASH YOUR CHECK.

Outside an Italian opera house: "TONIGHT: *THE BARBER OF SEVILLE.* 2,000 CHAIRS. NO WAITING".

Road sign: DRIVE CAREFULLY; DON'T INSIST UPON YOUR RITES.

In a reducing-salon window: WE CAN TAKE YOUR BREADTH AWAY.

Sign in an undertaker's window: DRIVE CAREFULLY — WE CAN WAIT.

In window of a strike-bound bar and grille: "CLOSED FOR ALTERCATIONS!"

Rest-room signs at a bar in hunting country: POINTERS; SETTERS.

By a Laundry: WE SOAK THE CLOTHES, NOT THE CUSTOMERS.

Outside a farm: FRESH EGGS BEING LAID NOW.

US of A

SOME ALL-AMERICAN GAGS

At a hick college with a fourth-rate faculty but a first-rate football team, the varsity fullback was a formidable brute who had just about enough sense to sit down when he was tired. Nevertheless, a determined English prof picked on him one morning to name three characters in Malory's classic *Le Morte d'Arthur.* The fullback pondered deeply, and then came up with a hopeful, "Well, first of all, I guess there was old Mort himself."

"Who," a precocious office boy dared to ask his boss, "were those two ladies I just ushered out of your office?" "One was my wife," joshed the indulgent boss, "and the other was Sophia Loren." "Which one was Loren?" asked the lad with a perfectly straight face.

The boss whipped a dollar bill out of his wallet and handed it to the office boy. "It's a loan," he explained. "When you succeed me as president, I want you to remember that I once loaned you money."

If the garbage workers in your community ever go out on strike you might like to know how a wise New Yorker disposed of his refuse for the nine days the sanitation workers were off the job last summer. Each day he wrapped his garbage in gift paper. Then he put it in a shopping bag. When he parked his car, he left the bag on the front seat with the window open. When he got back to the car the garbage always had been collected.

The politician was mangling and misusing the facts during his political tirade. "He's murdering the truth," said one newspaperman to another.

"Don't worry," said he. "He'll never get close enough to it to do it any harm."

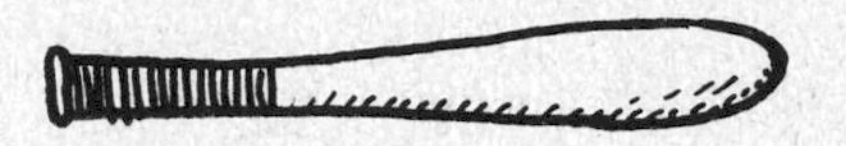

An elderly sinner renounced the world and sought sanctuary at a Trappist monastery, though he was warned by the Master of Novices he couldn't speak for five solid years—and then would be permitted only two words. At the end of the five years he reappeared before the Master and spoke his two words: "Hard beds!" Another five years drifted by, and now his two words were "Terrible food." At the end of the third five-year period, he announced, "I quit." "It's about time," nodded the Master of Novices. "All the time you've been here, you've done nothing but complain!"

Maybe you're under the impression that El Paso is the name of a big city in Texas. Wrong, asserts Johnny Carson. It's a Mexican football player who can neither el rusho or el punto.

THE FIELDS FORMULA FOR FRETTING FEMALES

7:00-8:00. Arise quietly, shake down furnace, stoke it, prepare breakfast — eggs exactly four minutes, two lumps of ice in the cocktail!
8:00-8:10. Awake husband gently, singing *sotto voce.* My preferences would be "Narcissus" or "Silent Night".
9:00-10:00. Drive husband to station, do shopping for dinner, and be sure not to order anything husband might decide to have for lunch.
10:00-12:00. Mow lawn, wash clothes, iron husband's shirts, press his suits, paint screens, weed garden, swat flies.
12:00-2:00. Clean cellar, wash windows, tidy house, beat rugs.
2:00-2:15. Eat simple lunch.
2:15-5:30. Spade garden, darn socks, wash Rover, put up jelly, polish car, burn rubbish, wash woodwork, paint garage, clean side walls of tires.
5:30-7:00. Drive to station for husband, shake cocktails, cook dinner, serve dinner, wash dishes.
7:00-2:00. Keep busy — keep smiling — for, as every man knows, the husband is tired.

I think, my friends, that *that* just about covers the subject of marriage.

YOU DIDN'T SEE ME AND I DIDN'T SEE YOU – ALRIGHT?

CANAJAN EH?

Since it is a bilingual country Canada has four languages. This gives fullest scope to linguistic self-expression while considerably increasing the likelihood of misunderstanding . . . On the French Canajan side, the fishle language is French . . . Most French Canajans, while they read and write French, talk Joual, the nash null language of Quebec . . . On the English Canajan side the fishle language is English, . . . Most English Canajans, although they are able to write English, talk Canajan, the nash null language of English Canada. As with Joual, no formal instruction in Canajan is either given or necessary. Who would need it? All Anglos speak Canajan from birth.

(You've just got to say the words slowly until suddenly you get it — we hope!)

ARSEY EM PEE: A para-military police body combining the most distinctive features of the army (red coats), the civil service (red tape), the secret service (Red hunting) and politics (red herrings). Also known as 'The Moundies'.

ASBESTOS: To the extent of your ability. As in: *'You'll haveta make do asbestos you can.'*

BEARUS: To disconcert. As in: *'Twuz reely bearussing ta seer there.'*

BERREX: Buildings where soldiers were lodged.

BRIDDISH: Of or pertaining to Grade Bridden. Sometimes contracted to Brish, as in: Brish Commwealth.

COMMA NIZZUM: System of social organization, particularly as developed by Marks and Lennon. The opposite of Free Dumb, q.v.

DIE JEST OF TRACK: the place inside people, animals, etc. where things turn into other things.

EGG SPURT: Someone with special skill or knowledge.

by Morkin Orkin, published by General Pub. Co. Ontario

FEBBOO WARY: The month following Jannery.

HAN CHA: Interrogative phrase used to ascertain the availability of something. As in: *'Han cha gottiny matches, Rick?'*

IMM GRUNT: One who comes into the country as a seddler . . .

JOGGA FEE: Study of the earth's features, population, climb it etc.

MAZKIDDA: The nash null insect of Canada. A kind of gnat whose bite causes a prolonged itching sensation. . . .

PERALIZED: Crippled, rendered powerless.

SENNER: The middle point . . .

STRUCK SHIRLEY: Of or pertaining to building. As in: 'The howsiz struck shirley sound.' . . .

YOGODDINY: Interrogative to ascertain the availability of something. As in: *'Yagoddiny ornjuz? melk? etc.'*

ZARRITE: Interrogative response to an affirmative verbal statement, often indicating mild disbelief. As in: *'Susan, Ike ud reely gopher you!' 'Zarrite?'.*

"Please sit down and await your turn."

"What's the use of hanging around here? They only give it to you if you're sick."

"I'm worried about him, doctor. He hasn't said a word for weeks."

Cartoons from 'When Did You Last Clean Your Navel? by James Simpkins published by Potlatch Pubcns., Ontario

NEWFIE, COME HOME

What have the Irishman, the Pollak, and the Newfie got in common? They're all dumb, that's what — at least, when it comes to jokes. And the Newfie, in case you don't already know, is the Newfoundlander, the odd ball on the Canadian scene — the bloke they hang all the dimmest punch lines on. Which doesn't stop Newfies thinking that (and I quote) there are only two kinds of people in this world—Newfoundlanders and thems that wishes they wuz.

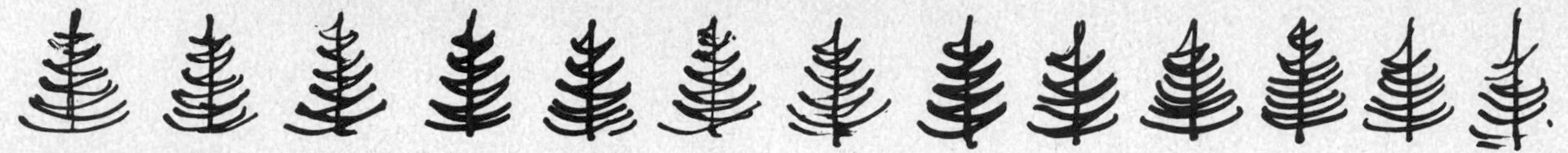

My grandfather drank a bottle of rum every day since he was seventeen years old. He died nine years ago at the age of eighty, was cremated and they're still trying to put the fire out.

Did you hear about the Newfie who was stranded on an island with three girls for nine years? When they were found, the only words he could say were "eenie", "meenie", "minie".

After just getting discharged from the navy, a Newfie, a Nova Scotian and a Torontonian decided to stay in England for a few weeks. They went on one hell of a drunk and woke up one morning, about two weeks later, with a hangover and not a cent in their pockets. They were outside an exclusive bar when the Nova Scotian got an idea. He went into the bar and ordered a double rum. When he had finished, the barman said: "That will be two dollars, sir." Nova Scotian: "I paid you." Barman: "No sir, you did not." Nova Scotian, in a loud voice: "I darn well did pay you." Barman whispered: "Ok, please don't disturb the customers."

When the Nova Scotian got outside he told his buddies what had happened so the Torontonian went in and did the same thing. Newfie went in after, ordered a double rum and the barman said: "You know, just before you got here, two other fellows came in and ordered double rums. They swore that they paid me, but for the life of me I can't remember them doing so." Newfie: "Listen, pal, you got your problems and I got mine. Just give me the change from my twenty so I can get the hell out of here."

Two Newfie astronauts went to the moon. (That should be a joke in itself). One of them stayed inside the ship to cook a meal of fish and brewis while the other went out collecting rocks. When the rock collector returned, he knocked on the door and the fellow inside said, "Who's there?"

A MOUNTY ALWAYS GETS HIS MAN!

A Torontorian walked into the barber shop and asked: "How come your hands are so dirty, today?"

Newfie: "You're the first to get a shampoo today."

Newfie: "How much are your eggs?"

Nova Scotian: "Ninety cents for whole and forty cents for the cracked ones."

Newfie: "Crack me two dozen, will ya."

Yank: "Why do birds fly south?"
Newfie: "Too far to walk, I guess."

Excerpts from 'Newfie Joke Books' by Bob Tulk, Published by Newfie Jokes

GOON FOR LUNCH

HARRY SECOMBE

Court Usher: Do you swear to tell the truth, the whole truth and nothing but the truth?

Seagoon: Yes.

Usher: You're going to be in a right mess then, mate.

This little extract from a Spike Milligan Goon Show script seems to sum up rather succinctly the prevalent attitude towards honesty. We live in the age of the half truth, the slightly bent statistic and the party manifesto, which is a combination of the other two.

One can only write honestly about honesty where it applies to oneself and one's relations with others; so, on the somewhat overworked premise that the child is father of the man, let us look into some of my own youthful encounters with the truth. It's not a pretty sight, I warn you.

When I was a lad I was an avid reader of Arthur Mee's *Children's Newspaper* and *True Confessions.* The first was ordered for us by our parents and the second was read clandestinely when they were out. One was full of tales of honour and Empire and biographies of people like Philip Sydney and Edith Cavell, and the other told of dishonour and seduction, never explicit but hinted at by delicious dots. I must admit that I found the exploits of Mrs X of Trenton, New Jersey far more exciting than the tribulations of St Francis of Assisi, who must have spent too much time trying to get the bird lime off his habit to have naughty dishonest thoughts.

However, we were brought up in the belief that it was better to tell the truth and face the consequences than to tell a lie. As a choirboy I remember sitting through a sermon on this theme, nodding sagely with my Young Woodley face on, my mind switching rapidly from thoughts of what was for lunch to agonised speculation on whether I should tell my mother about being caught playing doctors and nurses with Jessie Probert by her elder sister who now showed signs of wishing to be examined herself. At twelve years of age I was too young to cope with a full surgery, and was avoiding both girls, who, to my mother's surprise, had taken to calling at our house and asking if I could come out to play. I was a junior Dr Jekyll who was forced to hide. I was saved from a head-on confrontation with the truth by a fortuitous bout of yellow jaundice, during which I abandoned *True Confessions* and settled instead for a less heady diet of *Film Fun* and *The Magnet.* Just after my illness the Probert sisters discovered an embryonic gynaecologist living in the next street, and I was spared their attentions.

A Milker in the Mail

By
PATRICK CAMPBELL

Riffling through my souvenirs in search of a prescription for vertigo, I came upon a short paragraph roughly hacked from an American magazine.

It's an extract from Ripley — 'Believe It or Not' — and it announces a new wonder of the world.

John L. Lunnon, of Well End Farm, Buckinghamshire, sent a live cow to market by post.

Even after an interval of some years, the cutting causes me a thin smile. John L. Lunnon sent it, did he? You might as well say that Enid Blyton wrote *Look Back in Anger,* that *Lolita* was the brain-child of Wilhelmina Stitch.

I was the poster of that cow, the first man in the history of the world to do so, and I want to say that there was nothing to it. It was a down-hill trot, nearly all the way.

Let's marshal the facts.

The business was started by Mr. Ernest Marples, at that time the Assistant Postmaster-General, during the course of a speech to some gathering whose identity I forget. Mr. Marples, always a buoyant publicist for his own department, said that the Post Office was ready to post anything anywhere. Even, he added — probably at random — a cow.

I have to admit that the report whipped me up into no great lather. It seemed to be no more than routine, after-luncheon jollity, and I passed on to some more interesting matter on the next page. It wasn't in fact, until the following day that I saw its real potential, in the course of a conversation with my employer, Mr. Charles Eade, who was then editing the *Sunday Dispatch.* I retain a clear recollection of the dialogue.

'Good morning. Got any ideas?'

'No, sir. Not yet.'

'I see that Marples says you can post a cow.'

'Yes, sir. I saw that.'

'Well, then — go and post one.'

'Yes, sir.'

I didn't like the look of it at all. The project was beset with difficulties, not the least of which was to find a postable cow. Then I took heart. A single telephone call to any post office would surely reveal that Mr. Marples, in the heat of oratory, had gone too far. I might even get a column on the familiar theme of bureaucratic confusion, with the workers struggling to keep up with the impractical boastings of the boss.

I suddenly remembered that my village post office was also called the Parade Dairy — an ideal branch in which to fail to post a cow. I called upon the sub-postmaster, a brisk young man called Browne, with whom I'd already had some amusing chats about arrears of National Health stamps (self-employed).

'Afternoon, Mr. Browne. I want to post a cow.'

'To post a cow, sir?' He was polite and unsmiling, wary — I thought — of some ham-handed practical joke.

'Mr. Marples says you can post cows. I just wanted to put it to the test.'

'I see, sir. Do you mind waiting a moment while I check with head office in Maidenhead?'

I followed him into the inner part of the shop, to listen to the telephone call.

'Hello — Bourne End sub-post office here. I have a gentleman who wishes to post a cow.' Short pause. 'Thank you very much.' Mr. Browne put down the receiver. 'That will be perfectly all right, sir. The animal can be dispatched where and when you wish.' Not a trace of a smile. The head slightly on one side, waiting for my further pleasure.

'Thank you, Mr. Browne. I'll be back. I just have to get in touch with a cow —'

I guessed what had happened. As soon as Marples shot off his neck the GPO must have got in touch with every post office in the land, warning them to stand by for cow-posters. One up — again — to the Establishment.

The position was serious. Cow-posting was on, Mr. Eade desired it, but I hadn't got a cow. Then I remembered that the field over my boundary fence was infested with cows belonging to John Lunnon, with whom I'd already had some tart conversations about the injuries that might be sustained by cows stuck in vital places by golf balls.

I approached him with caution.

'John, would you like to post one of your cows?'

'Post it — where to?'

It was an aspect of the matter I hadn't yet contemplated.

'Well, anywhere you'd like one of your cows to go.'

He thought for a moment. 'There's a market at Bracknell this week.'

'The very place. Nice and handy.'

'On the other hand, it's not a good time to sell. I'd get more later.'

It was no time for cheeseparing. 'The *Sunday Dispatch* will make up the difference.'

He considered the matter again.

'Do they actually put a stamp on them?'

I saw he was hooked. 'I'm sure they do — right on the rump.'

He suddenly rubbed his hands. 'Let's post a cow.'

Unbelievably, the whole thing had fallen sweetly into place. I rang Charles Eade.

'Sir—the cow-posting's all sewn up! I've got a cow to post and a post office to post it from! We're ready to go!'

'Oh, that,' he said. 'Well, just make sure it doesn't get slaughtered. A lot of our animal-loving readers wouldn't like to think we'd taken a cow out of a field, and posted it to its death.'

'No, sir. Of course not.'

'Good-bye.'

I didn't mention the matter of Bessie's possible fate as John and I closed in on her the following morning, in a corner of the field. I already had a clear picture — captioned — in my mind of a rubicund old farmer who, overjoyed to find himself the owner of the world's first posted cow, put her out to grass in a special paddock for the rest of her life, with a notice on the gate underlining her distinction.

The Post Office van, when it arrived to take delivery of the parcel, was a set-back. It wasn't red and it didn't carry the royal insignia. It was, in fact, just an ordinary lorry with a ramp, chartered from a private haulier. But in attendance there was a representative from the GPO — an apprehensive telegraph boy on a motor-cycle, wearing uniform, a crash helmet and goggles. He looked about thirteen. Probably the older and wiser lads at Maidenhead head office had stuck him with the job by general consent.

He regarded us warily. 'Orders,' he said in the end, 'to collect an item for delivery —'

'It's in there,' I said. 'Breathing.'

It was clear that Bessie didn't know she was making history, because it took the four of us to post her up the ramp and into the lorry. For the record, she was a thin, brown-and-white cow with a curiously prim disposition. I was sorry we hadn't got a cow that entered more into the spirit of the thing.

The telegraph boy didn't like her either. Post office regulations, it seemed, compelled him to accompany her from the point of dispatch to the place of delivery. He abandoned his motor-bike with obvious regret and climbed into the front seat of the lorry beside the driver, still wearing his crash helmet and goggles. When I suggested that he should, strictly speaking, be in the back, with Bessie, he said, 'Do me a favour, willya?'

No extra sparkle was provided by our first call, at the Parade Dairy sub-post office. John and I were reversing Bessie with the intention of pushing her, for stamping, as far into the shop as she would go, when Mr. Browne appeared with a small buff form. It was only necessary, it seemed, for me to sign it, and to pay the parcel post charges, and then Bessie could be on her way.

A small crowd had gathered, seeing a cow being pushed into the post office. A lady with shopping basket was kind enough to stick a 7p stamp on Bessie's forehead, and to wish us luck, but there was no further public demonstration. We beat Bessie back into the lorry again, and started for Bracknell.

Here, things were rather livelier. Word of the enterprise had clearly preceded us, because there was quite a posse of press photographers, mostly from local newspapers. The telegraph boy and I, with Bessie in the middle, posed for a number of pictures on the ramp, until a representative of the auctioneer appeared to say that we were holding up the business of the market, and would we kindly get the lorry out of that.

Somewhat cast down by the increasingly chilly reception being accorded to our glorious, posted cow, John and I went into the pub next door, having discovered that Bessie would come up for auction at about two o'clock.

We emerged at 1.45, to find that Bessie had already been sold for £40, which was about right.

On second thoughts, now that I've marshalled the facts, I don't mind so much about Ripley giving all the credit to John L. Lunnon for posting a live cow.

Viewed in the round, it seems a pretty filthy thing to do.

Excerpt from '35 Years On The Job' by Patrick Campbell published by Blond & Briggs Ltd.

The Daily Blooper

MALE or FEMALE TRAINEE SPONGERS

Number of Young Persons required as Trainee Spongers. This is an opportunity to acquire pottery skills and to work within an expanding company.

Telephone our Personnel Manager for an interview appointment. Telephone S.O.T. 261031.

TAUNTON VALE INDUSTRIES LTD.
NORFOLK STREET, SHELTON

Stoke-on-Trent Evening Sentinel

FOR SALE
Health resort 240 acres in clear Vermont air. Two main buildings, 20 cabins plus 8 whirlpool and Sauna baths. Heated swimming pool, hot springs and mineral baths. Organic foods franchise and drug store with complete inventory and registered pharmacist in charge. $250,000 *Must sell due to ill health.*

—Benton Falls (Vt.) Advocate

MILK RACE

It's a strong strategic base for next week's operation, but unfortunately Bayton, who would have been Edwards's natural deputy, is still suffering from his fall. He finished at New Brighton with the bunch, but his back still pains, and he felt every hum in the road.

It was Havelka, a Czech of whom we know very little, who opened . . .

Observer

THERE'S more to being an MP's wife than just attending coffee mornings and opening fetes, as I discovered when I called on Mrs Betty Harrison, wife of Maldon MP Mr Brian Harrison, at Copford Hall, her very English home in the midst of the Essex countryside.

Mrs Harrison is friendly, likeable and easy to talk to. Her dark hair is attractively set, and she has fine fair skin, which, she admits ruefully, comes out in "a mass of freckles" at the first hint of sin.

Her husband is away in London from Monday to Thursday most weeks,

Essex County Standard

No. 69 One Pair Unique 18th cent. Candlesticks.
No. 70 Another Pair, ditto.

Auctioneer's catalogue

IRRESISTIBLE. That is what a 63-year-old man thought when a mini-skirted girl sat next to him on a bus. He bit her thigh. And was jailed for three days at Belo Horizonte, Brazil. His comment: 'The Pope was right. Mini-skirts are dangerous.'

Weekly paper

WIDOW IN BED WITH A CASE OF SALMON, CITY COURT TOLD

Liverpool Echo

Amazing luck in the Irish Sweep fell to a Kentish man who drew two tickets and a Sussex woman.

Yorkshire paper

The mayor apologized for the remarks attributed to him in the newspapers saying he had been completely misquoted. He had not said that recipients of welfare were lechers and parasites. His actual words had been "leeches and parasites."

—IRVINGTON (MD.) DEMOCRAT

[*That should smooth some ruffled fathers!*]

The retiring police commissioner has been responsible for all crimes committed in the district for the past twenty years.

—WEMBLEY (VA.) NEWS

Pink Panther case of unseen bullet holes

By C. A. COUGHLIN, Old Bailey Correspondent

A DOCTOR called in to examine a dead butler with five bullet wounds in his head decided death was from natural causes, an Old Bailey jury was told yesterday.

Three policemen also present were not suspicious either, said Mr MICHAEL NELIGAN, prosecuting.

Mr Shubini had two bullet wounds in the back of his head two through the side of his head and one fired at pointblank range through the forehead.

Dr MICHAEL HARDING, of Knightsbridge—in evidence read by Mr Neligan—stated: "I saw a dead man and detected no obvious cause of death."

STIRRUP TEASE

A horse was about to remove a strip-tease dancer's underwear with his teeth as part of a Bonn night club act when a customer attracted the animal's attention with a lump of sugar and rode off down the street.—Reuter.

THE acoustics of the cathedral have improved tremendously since 1896. In those days, the voluminous skirts of the female parishioners absorbed much of the volume of sound but now with the advent of the miniskirt the old organ really goes to town.

—GRANADA (MINN.) STAR

DEAD-PAN HUMOUR

Being funny, as any good comedian will tell you, can be a serious business — and by that token, being funny about kicking the bucket, passing over — or whatever euphemism takes your particular fancy — is something else again. Trouble is, and unlike any other jokey situation, it not only can — but is going to — happen to you one of these days. Which — if you're kinky like me — doesn't so much depress as give several extra zings to the living I'm here to enjoy right now. So "salut, la platta, y amore" as a Uruguyan duellist once said to me (and you can jolly well look that up in a Spanish dictionary — just as I did, in case he'd said something rude) — and long may it last:

K.B.

I believe I heard tell recently that there's a move afoot to clamp down on all the elaborately carved gravestones and fancifully worded epitaphs which up till now we've been free to compose and set up for our loved ones. Shame on Them — whoever they may be — and I'll fight to the death (marvellous, isn't it, how the right turn of phrase comes up) to preserve our right to perpetrate lovely last words like these:

The Daily Blooper

MR. JONES is wrong to suggest that I support the rich against the poor. To the Christian there is no class distinction—that idea was largely concocted by the working classes.

Letter in *Reynolds News*

The Government were strongly urged to take steps to put a stop to the growing evil of methylated spirit drinking by the Liverpool justices at their quarterly meetings.

Liverpool paper

An inscribed leather suitcase was presented to Mrs Ashton, a pipe to Mrs Longmore, and Mrs Hersey also received gifts. Mr Walter Painter received a knock from a cricket ball which fractured a bone in his hand.

Australian paper

WANTED: Man to work on nuclear fissionable isotope molecular reactive counters and three-phase cyclotronic uranium photo synthesizers. No experience necessary.

Advert in *The Mines Magazine*

Amid the cheers of their many friends in the farming community the bride and groom cut the wedding cake made by Mrs Luston (shaped like a haystack on stilts).

Dayton, Ohio, paper quoted in *Evening Standard*

Arrested for assault after hijacking a policeman at knifepoint by jumping on his back and ordering him "To walk to Cuba", an unnamed New Yorker was characterised by his arresting officer as "some kind of a nut. He fainted when I told him it meant three refuelling stops."

Not to be outdone by other artists, John Totten and his banjo along with several friends and their banjos will provide an instrumental interlude which itself should be worth the price of admission (which by the way is free).

Massachusetts paper

AT the fair they will be exhibiting a full range of shoes for girls with low-cut fancy uppers.

Leicester Mercury

When examined by the Divisional Surgeon, defendant was very abusive and when asked to clench his teeth, he took them out, gave them to the doctor and said, 'You clench them.'

Woking Herald & News

A man, alleged to have been caught stealing six chickens from a butcher's shop, was said to have told the police: 'I was taking them home to throw at the wife. We've had a row.'

News of the World

A very enjoyable affair was the Children's Hallowe'en Party. Added to the beauty of it all was the fact that few of the children could be recognized as they all wore masks.

Jamaican paper

Manuel Walters of the Malay Mob awoke in a temper. His anger was caused by the six .22 bullets which had thudded into him as he slept.

Drum

All this is being investigated today by the Scottish Society for the Prevention of Cruelty to Animals and Glasgow police.

Glasgow Evening Times

THERE are also the universities, in which it is estimated that one person in 1150 is educated.

Northumberland paper

At the end of the two-hour itinerary, refreshments were provided by Ready-Mix Concrete Ltd.

Eastwood and Kimberley Advertiser

Marinade the steak in the sauce for at least two hours, then cook a hot grill, basting with the sauce at frequent intervals. Alternatively, pour off sauce after marinading, heat separately, and let your guests pour it over themselves.

Recipe in Ohio newspaper

The marriage suffered a setback in 1965 when the husband was killed by the wife.

The New Law Journal

From

JAKE'S—PROGRESS

LEOPOLD ALCOCKS

Leopold Alcocks, my distant relation,
Came to my flat for a brief visitation.
He's been here since February, damn and blast him
My nerves and my furniture may not outlast him.

Leopold Alcocks is accident prone.
He's lost my bath plug, he's ruptured my telephone.
My antirrhinums, my motor bike, my sofa
There isn't anything he can't trip over.

As he roams through my rooms, all my pussycats scatter.
My statuettes tremble, then plummet, then shatter.
My table lamps tumble with grim regularity.
My cut glass has crumbled and so has my charity.

Leopold Alcocks, an uncanny creature
He can't take tea without some misadventure:
He looks up from his tea cup with a smirk on his features
And a slice of my procelain between his dentures.

He's upset my goldfish, he's jinxed my wisteria
My budgie's gone broody, my tortoise has hysteria.
He cleans my tea pots, my saucepans, with Brasso
And leaves chocolate finger prints on my Picasso.

Leopold Alcocks never known to fail
Working his way through my frail Chippendale.
One blow from his thighs (which are fearsomely strong)
Would easily fracture the wing of a swan.

I brought home my bird for some turkish moussaka
Up looms old Leopold I know when I'm knackered.
He spills the vino, the great eager beaver,
Dher jump suit and my joie de vivre.

Leopold Alcocks stirring my spleen
You are the grit in my life's vaseline.
A pox on you Alcocks! You've been here since Feb'ry
Go home and leave me alone with my debris.

So Leopold Alcocks, my distant relation,
Has gone away home after his visitation.
I glimpsed him waving bye bye this last minute
Waving his hand with my door knob still in it.

1.

WORRIED BROWN EYES

She always signs her letters Worried Brown Eyes,
The queen of every problem page at seventeen;
Never a week goes by but Worried Brown Eyes
Is hanging out her heart-achings in the ladies' weekly magazine.
She has got a boyfriend, name of Dickie,
Who would like to go too far;
(You know what Dickies are.)
And she is asking is he honourable or is he just a prancing Don Juan
But worse of all she fears
Could she love a man who picks his ears?

She always signs her letters Worried Brown Eyes
She says she's got a little mole
In a place where nobody's ever seen
And she asks "Is it unsightly?" pretty Brown Eyes,
Seeking advice on mole control in the ladies' weekly magazine.
Then of course there's Dickie, desperate Dickie
Who is growing very bold
(His hands are so cold!)
Well now's your chance, oh little Brown Eyes,
To be passionate and rash and indiscreet;
Body and soul
Go on, give the lad a treat; show him your mole.

She always signs her letters Worried Brown Eyes
Revealing every secret of her shy hygiene;
She'd like a bigger bosom Worried Brown Eyes
Thrashing out her tummy bulges in the ladies weekly magazine.
Dickie's been molesting her and pestering her again,
He is obsessed,
He gives her no rest
Every letter's full of Tricky Dickie
But this week I feel there's something new;
He must have made his move
Something must have happened: her handwriting's improved.

Oh spare some kind of prayer for Worried Brown Eyes,
Queen of every problem page at seventeen
Never a week goes by but Worried Brown Eyes
Is hanging out her desperations in the ladies' weekly magazine.

Would she do it? Could she do it? Should she?
Opening up her heart-aching so ill-advisedly;
Brown eyes that nobody's ever seen,
With her Dickie-di-do, in the ladies' weekly magazine.

2.

Excerpts from 'Jake's Progress' by Jake Thackray published by W. H. Allen & Co. Ltd.

Confucius he Say

"Nothing succeeds like excess." Oscar Wilde

"If you see a snake coming toward you in a jungle, you have a right to be anxious; if you see it coming down Park Avenue, you're in trouble." Theodor Reik

"Sit with a pretty girl for an hour, and it seems like a minute; sit on a hot stove for a minute, and it seems like an hour—that's relativity." Albert Einstein

"When some men discharge an obligation, you can hear the report for miles around." Mark Twain

"When you are down and out, something always turns up—and it is usually the noses of your friends." Orson Welles

"To err is human, but it feels divine." Mae West

"I must be getting old because nowadays I find I'm more interested in the food I eat than in the girl who serves it." John Steinbeck

"One way to solve the traffic problem would be to keep all the cars that are not paid for off the streets." Will Rogers

"Wise men talk because they have something to say; fools, because they have to say something " Plato

"It's not the men in my life that counts—its the life in my men." Mae West

"It is the plain women who know about love; the beautiful women are too busy being fascinating." Katherine Hepburn

"A woman may be as wicked as she likes but if she isn't pretty, it won't do her much good." Somerset Maugham

"He practised the utmost economy in order to keep up the most expensive habits." George Bernard Shaw

"Let the meek inherit the earth—they have it coming to them." James Thurber

"There is no such thing as a little garlic." Arthur Baer

"A fanatic is one who can't change his mind and won't change the subject." Winston Churchill

"All tragedies are finished by death; all comedies are ended by a marriage." Lord Byron

"The best service a retired general can perform is to turn in his tongue along with his suit." General Omar Bradley